Helion & Company Limited
Unit 8 Amherst Business Centre
Budbrooke Road
Warwick
CV34 5WE
England
Tel. 01926 499 619
Email: info@helion.co.uk
Website: www.helion.co.uk
Twitter: @helionbooks
Visit our blog http://blog.helion.co.uk/

Designed & typeset by Farr out Publications, Wokingham, Berkshire
Cover design by Paul Hewitt, Battlefield Design (www.battlefield-design.co.uk)

Front cover: The Saharan honour guard unit pays tribute to the commander of the MINURSO military contingent, Major General György Száraz, who first visited the SADR-supervised 'Liberated zone' in 2002. (János Besenyő collection)

ISBN 978-1-804512-06-7

British Library Cataloguing-in-Publication Data
A catalogue record for this book is available from the British Library

We always welcome receiving book proposals from prospective authors.

CONTENTS

Note: In order to simplify the use of this book, all names, locations and geographic designations are as provided in *The Times World Atlas*, or other traditionally accepted major sources of reference, as of the time of described events.

Acronyms and Abbreviations

BCE	Before Common Era (formerly referred to as BC/ Before Christ)
BIS	Independent Infantry Battalions
CE	Common Era (formerly referred to as AD/Anno Domini)
GPS	Global Positioning System
MINURSO	*Mission des Nations Unies pour l'Organization d'un Referendum au Sahara Occidental* (United Nations Mission for the Referendum in Western Sahara)
NATO	North Atlantic Treaty Organisation
OAU	Organization of African Unity
POLISARIO	Popular Front for the Liberation of Saguia el-Hamra and Río de Oro/*Frente Popular para la Liberación de Saguia el Hamra y Río de Oro* (also often written Polisario)
SADR	Sahrawi Arab Democratic Republic
SRSG	Special Representative of the UN Secretary-General
UNHCR	United Nations High Commissioner for Refugees
US	United States

Introduction

This book is intended to be a part of a series of works that have been published about themes of warfare and conflicts under the auspices of Helion & Company Limited. In accordance with the previous issues which concern the various aspects of military warfare in different countries or situations, the current text tries to live up to the expectations of the high quality provided so far by the series.

Following tradition, the next pages will be dedicated to the history and structure of the peacekeeping mission MINURSO (United Nations Mission for the Referendum in Western Sahara). The author would like to take into consideration all important aspects of the mission, from the history of Western Sahara up to the design of the organisation and its other aspects.

First and foremost, it is important to declare that the literature regarding the issue is not abundant, however, it was the sincere intention of the writer to produce a scientifically neutral, thorough understanding of the issue on the grounds of the best sources that were possible to obtain. The book intends to present an image of the conflict from a quite independent view of the events, and the author seeks to demonstrate the background and the circumstances of the mission in the best possible way.

The author has tried to use as many publications and resources as possible to provide evidence regarding the outlook of the mission, and to be able to present for the average reader the important aspects of the conflict and the organisation which tries to contribute to the solution of a very complex regional problem that actually involves the whole Maghreb area.

Nevertheless, besides its scientific value, this text aims to be of interest to the average reader and tries to pass onto that person the interesting events and issues that concern the mission and its background. The author hopes that at the end this book will become an interesting source both for the academics interested in the scarcely researched theme and for the average person who simply wants to understand the conflict and the mission trying to solve it.[1]

1
A Brief Historical Background to MINURSO: The Western Saharan Conflict

Geography of Western Sahara

Western Sahara is situated in the north-western part of Africa, right at the gate of the Mediterranean Sea. Its area is 266,000km^2 and it is a smooth, monotonous landscape with vast deserts and a few occasional lower peaks. It lies directly beneath the Atlas Mountains of Morocco, and it is encircled by higher mountains in the far distance.[1] Thanks to the desert climate, the area is filled with sand which supports few animals and only sparse vegetation. The highest point of the country is at 721 metres, while its lowest is Sebhet Taj at 55 metres. No matter how enormous the desert is, there are a few mountainous areas which colour the otherwise unchanged desert hills.

There are a few oases, and the desert people, the Sahrawis, living in the area know some wells that can ease the scorching heat that permeates the environment of the region. Western Sahara comprises of three different zones, separable according to their climate and their environmental characteristics. The first is called the *hamadas*, and it is a mixture of mountainous and desertic lands. It is situated in the northern quadrant of the country, ranging from the Atlas third of the area. Heading further south, one finds oneself in a more fruitful region, which is called the Saguia el-Hamra – this area bears the title of one of its largest rivers and it refers to the relatively denser water sources, thus in this place agriculture can develop a little. The southernmost part of Western Sahara is named Río de Oro, which is a great desert area divided by hills. It has some water sources, and

Mountainous area of Western Sahara. (János Besenyő collection)

Hamadas of Western Sahara. (János Besenyő collection)

it is a very colourful region. In summary, the area is a vast desert filled with smaller hills and some oases with a very few animals and little vegetation. The climate is very hot, the temperature can reach more than 50 degrees C and there is minimal rainfall in the area. The wind is also a problem because it obstructs mobility and movement in the territory.[2]

Early History of Western Sahara

The area today known as Western Sahara was a remote and unknown part of the ancient world. There are some signs, in the form of rock engravings, of primitive culture existing in prehistoric times. There are signs of the emergence of rudimentary human civilisation in the Stone Age and of Homo habilis, Homo erectus and finally, Homo sapiens. The latter group appeared in the region by 12,000 BCE and from then on, the development of tools, jewellery and weapons began. By 4,000 BCE, the Neolithic culture appeared and in these millennia three elements converged in the area – a negro civilisation, a culture from the Sudan area, and an indigenous Saharan tradition that has emerged in the wake of the new events.[3] The inhabitants of the desertic region became the so-called Bafour, who were a black people, and settled in the area before the Berber people arrived there. The Bafour raised cattle, created a pastoral living and led an agricultural life. The monuments that remind us of that period consist of rock paintings and artifacts which mostly depict wild African animals of that area. At that time, the territory was not as desertous as today, and the indigenous black tribes and Berber people were mainly concerned with animal husbandry and agriculture.[4] This lasted until 3,000 BCE, when a serious drying of the climate occurred.

This had irreversible consequences for the population living in the area and it started a millennia-long migration of the people there, since the conditions for agriculture had changed, because the weather became harsher and it was no longer possible for the sedentary black inhabitants to continue their peaceful agricultural life in the former savannah areas, which became deserts. Thus, a new, more violent group of people emerged in the area, who came from the Atlas Mountains from the north – these were the Berbers. They were equipped with iron weapons and horses and had the advantage in conflict with the Bafour and drove them away from the Saharan lands to the south.[5]

Near 1,000 BCE, the area was conquered by the Phoenicians, who sent several missions to the area by water or on land. For example, Hanno the Great went on an expedition to the area wishing to get around the western side of the African coast all the way to the area of Western Sahara in the fifth century BCE (although the exact date is not certain).[6] The area, however, remained unexplored and was still a blank space on the maps of the empires that sought the gold of southern Africa.

The next big change in the life of the Saharan nomads was the arrival of the camel and it replacing the horse in the culture of the nomads, an animal recorded in the first century BCE by the

Mreira well. (János Besenyő collection)

Coast of Western Sahara at Dakhla. (János Besenyő collection)

Romans.[7] It is needless to say that the appearance of this animal gave possibility to life in the desert environment, so the nomadic tribes began to dwell in these areas.

The next phase in the history of the area came with the rise of the Roman Empire, who also colonised the Maghreb area despite not really being able to get to the present area of Western Sahara. After them, first the Vandals, then the Byzantines occupied the region, but seem to have had no strong influence on the life of the nomads.[8] The first big blow came directly after the spread of Islam from the Middle East. The rapid conquest by the Arabic-Muslim armies from the east in the seventh century CE was followed, of course, by the Islamification of the region. The soldiers of Islam – led by Umayyad Okba ben Nafi – conquered the area by 681 CE. After him, Moussa ben Nusair continued to secure the region for the vast Muslim empire, and in 711, he struck a decisive blow against the Berbers to ensure his reign in the area.[9] The customary and religious law of Islam, the Arabic language of the conquerors, and the cultural heritage that came with the advance of the eastern civilisation had its impact on the Saharan population, but it took centuries for it to take root in the minds of the nomad population, so it was not until the ninth century that it made its impact on the indigenous people. At that time there were two tribes of the Berber community who ruled the Western Maghreb region: the Zenata and the Sanhaja Berbers. The Zenata were concentrated more likely in the northern part of the area, in southern Morocco, while the Sanhaja Berbers lived to the south in the area of today's Western Sahara. The Sanhaja were competing with the remaining black population, which they drove southwards as they conquered the territories of the region. Still, at the same time, the Ghanaian Kingdom was at its peak and the two powers clashed for several decades. However, in the end the Sanhaja were victorious, and defeated the Soninke Empire of Ghana. At the same time, they also won a decisive victory over the northern Zenata Berbers, and under the banner of Abdallah Ibn Yasin, a pious and religious man, unified the territory from Ghana to Muslim Spain which they conquered at the same time. Yasin formed a group of religious followers, and he created the so-called 'al-Murabitun' (Almoravids). They were the first to unite the Berber and other tribes of North Africa and create a vast empire that stretched even across the Mediterranean Sea. However, in 1125 a new power came into being in the Atlas, and the so-called Masmuda Berbers revolted against the Almoravids – who struggled with internal difficulties – and took over the empire, becoming the Almohads, the next large entity across the region.[10]

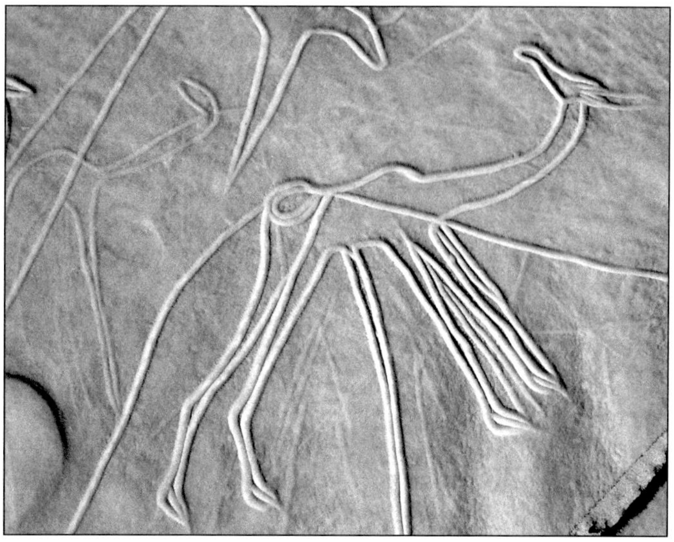

Rock carvings in Western Sahara showing giraffes. (János Besenyő collection)

For some time, little of importance occurred, but by 1218 a new tribe called the Maqil arrived in the desert areas of the Maghreb. These came from Yemen and were purely Arabic in descent. Soon after, one of its tribes – the Beni Hassan – migrated to the Western Saharan region and they started to mix with the Berbers, from which several tribes arose. One of the originally Arabic communities was the Oulad Delim, which preserved much of its Arabic heritage, however, other tribes, like the Tekna were composed more of Berber ethnicities.[11] These tribes came to dominate the Saharan territory, which thus became for several hundred years a practically independent area, where only the bravest adventurers and explorers dared to venture until the Spanish finally decided to colonise the interior of the area in the nineteenth and twentieth centuries.

Medieval History of Western Sahara

Medieval times brought about important changes in the life of the territory of today's Western Sahara. In the age of the great discoveries by European travellers the blank spaces on the maps always caused excitement and there was usually a patron to finance an expedition to explore the unknown areas of the world. It was no different with the Saharan land, which aroused special interest in the minds of the explorers. Before the era of Christopher Columbus and exploration of the Americas adventurers started to take interest in the West African region, which might have held precious goods and minerals that would be of interest to the various governments and leaders who sought wealth and dominance from the newly found territories.

There are records of travellers moving around the area even as early as the thirteenth and fourteenth centuries. Exploration started at an early point when in 1291, the Italian Vivaldi brothers visited the territory and find out about the so far relatively untouched coast, however, they failed to return from their journey. Soon there were others to follow: in approximately 1337, a wanderer named Mohamed ben Ragano reached Tidra Island, which lies in what is now Mauritania. He is one of the first people to have crossed the region to see the beauty of the desert and the ocean.[12] The Canary Islands appeared in the lists of travels first in 1309, and the next person who risked his life to explore the territory was Jaime Ferrer, who went on a long trip along the Saharan coast around 1346. The European explorers would gain a foothold in the territory in 1401, when they finally conquered the Canary Islands and began their long-lasting colonial activity along the shore, and later on the mainland of the continent.[13] The Europeans made several important discoveries they would later deem worthy of exploiting, but first of all, after the conquerors arrived at the Canary Islands, they almost immediately tried to explore the perilous coastlines of the continent opposite.

In 1405, Jean de Bethencourt went ashore near the Western Saharan region and went on to attack the Sahrawis – the indigenous people of later Western Sahara – and took several slaves. This became a preferred activity of the Europeans, who frequently visited the area to conduct the so-called *entradas* or slave campaigns. This continued until the time of the abolition of slavery and was a very profitable business for the assailants. However, they were also in search of gold and in a religious zeal to convert the Muslims and spread the word of Christianity.[14]

The first serious attempt to exploit and colonise these areas came from the Portuguese, namely Henry the Navigator, who from 1421 began several incursions into the area. Besides the usual benefits, he wanted to find another route to the Indies. His most famous adventure was conducted by the infamous Gil Eannes, who made a legendary trip into today's Western Sahara by sailing by the dangerous Cape Bojador which was impassable until then. Nevertheless, he wanted no more than the other colonising empires of that era: gold, slaves and other resources, and was motivated by religious zeal; Henry even obtained papal bulls to absolve him from sins against the indigenous Sahrawis, so the explorers could attack legitimately as knights who served their religion. The interior was however difficult, due to the sandy desertic climate, and the dry wind, and the conditions prevented the gaining of a foothold on the continent itself. The first base became the island of Arguin in 1448, which was to become the base of operations for the invaders for a long time to come.[15]

However, the Portuguese were not the only ones to lay eyes on the prize, since the Castilians (the Spanish) wanted their piece of the cake as well; it was then not unexpected that the Spanish invaders sought to establish for themselves an outpost on the continental part of Africa, which was done by Diego García de Herrera (governor of the Canary Islands), who established a fort on the coast of the mainland in 1476. The fort changed owner many times in the course of history, and it was a useful centre from which to start the *entradas*. The place was named Santa Cruz, and it became one of the most wanted posts on the coast.[16] There were also significant treaties that divided the spheres of interest in the region between Spain and Portugal. The most important of them was the Treaty of Tordesillas in 1494, which gave control of the coastal areas of today's Western Sahara to the Spanish. The fortress and the efforts of the European conquerors were deemed hostile by the Sahrawis, and so they declared jihad on them. The result was the capture of Santa Cruz, which changed owners again by the first half of the sixteenth century. Another important island was Arguin, which was first the possession of the Portuguese, but in 1638 a new power came on the scene: the Dutch, who captured the island.[17] However, Santa Cruz was not the only notable post in the desert area, since the Spanish sent another soldier, Alonso Fernandes De Lugo with the order to create three centres, from where the Spanish could continue their slave raids (Taghaost, San Miguel de Saca, Cape Bojador).[18] By this time, the European colonisation efforts had also brought about a religious fervour, namely the Inquisition, which tried to convert the locals to Christianity. These newly welcomed co-religionists were named the *moriscos*, who became interpreters, fishermen and the like. They however did not travel to Europe, because they wanted to stay in their homeland.[19]

The Early Modern Period of Western Sahara

After examining the European influence on the African coastline of Western Sahara, it is of equal value to take a brief look at the Moroccans, who lived in the vicinity of the Sahrawis. First of all, it is important to note that the lands Morocco ruled over were called *bilad al-makhzen*, and the southern parts, where the Sahrawis lived were named *bilad as-siba*. The latter was a distant country for the Moroccans, who could rarely impose even a limited dominance over the area. However, some of the tribes of the *bilad as-siba* agreed to sign contracts (*bayaa*) with the Moroccan rulers, who then granted them rights to become leaders in their regions. There were several dynasties in Morocco during the seventeenth and eighteenth centuries, one of them the Saadians. One of the Saadi rulers, Ahmed (son of one of the first rulers of the dynasty, Mohammed es-Sheikh) tried to pacify the Saharawis, with more or less success. After 1603, the country fell into turmoil, but in 1659, the most prominent Moroccan dynasty ascended the throne: they were the Alawites. One of their sultans, Moulay Ismail (1672–1727) was the most important ruler in their struggle to conquer the Western Saharan people, who had to obey his rule due to a large and powerful army. In spite of that, the Moroccan forces still could not claim the original parts of the Saharan lands. As time went on, British companies established a new trading post in Tarfaya and another in Sagiyat al Hamra. The sultans of Morocco in the nineteenth century continued their policy to pacify the *bilad as-siba* as they had before. Morocco also sought to stop the efforts of the colonising French and Spanish, though with little success.[20]

Before turning to the modern colonisation efforts of the Spanish and the French, it is perhaps interesting to take a look at various events and expeditions that took place from the sixteenth century until more recent times. One of the most remarkable phenomena was the island of Arguin, which has a unique history, though similar to that of the fort of Santa Cruz, as they both changed hands many times. By 1638, the Dutch were in charge of the island, but the English took it from them in 1665. Later, the Dutch recaptured this important location, but it was destroyed by the French in 1678. However, the Dutch were to return and reconquer the island in 1688, but the French were victorious in 1721 once more. This series of events kept on going for decades and the island was won by different powers alternately.

There were several expeditions in that age which aroused the interest of the world. A man named George Glas travelled in 1764 to Puerto Cansado. He then began to build a fort called Hilsborough, and in this fashion he widened the European influence over Western Sahara.[21] There were other interesting stories as well. For example, a man named Alexander Scott was captured by the nomads around Cape Juby between 1810 and 1816. His story is an interesting tale of the events he lived through in the area at the beginning of the nineteenth century.[22]

The Colonisation of Western Sahara

The next phase in the history of Western Sahara was the era of colonisation, mostly by the Spanish. After long discussions, in 1884 they submitted their claim to the territory of the Sahrawis.[23] It was accepted by the Berlin Conference in 1885 and Spain began to explore the area with the support of King Alphonso XII. There were two attempts to explore the Saharan area, but the more interesting route was taken by Emilio Bonelli Hernando who reached Dakhla, where he established a stronghold. In 1886, with the help of a large fleet, the Spanish landed on the shore of the Saharan lands and occupied the territory. However, the Sahrawis were not happy with the Spanish invasion, began a revolt against the colonising power, and attacked Villa Cisneros in 1887 and in 1892. With the resistance of the Saharan people rising to its height, the Spanish had another problem to settle. They had to come to terms with the French in order to delineate the borders between the Spanish-controlled Sahara and the French-controlled Morocco and Mauritania. These agreements were concluded in 1900, in 1904, and lastly in 1912. With these accords, the Madrid government secured for itself the areas at hand.[24] Because of these challenges Spain began negotiations with the Austro-Hungarian Monarchy on the possible sale of their African colony, Río de Oro, acquired in 1884. The colony was offered for rent or purchase to the Austro-Hungarian Colonial Society (*Österreich-Ungarische Kolonial-Gesellschaft*), founded in 1895. However, the Society alone was unable to take over the area, so it contacted the Ministry of Commerce of the Monarchy and also the Ministry of Foreign Affairs. The ministries of the Austro-Hungarian Monarchy found the offer tempting and joined the negotiations, which went on for more than a year, but the interested parties could not reach an agreement. In the end the Spaniards did not sell their colony but tried to strengthen their positions.[25]

The fight for the ownership of the Saharan area that helped the Spanish to secure the territory for themselves began between the French and a religious, educated saint-like figure, Ma el Ainin, whose real name was Mohamed Mustafa. When he appeared, the French

Casa del Mar (House of the Sea) is a fortress and trade point built by the Scottish explorer Donald MacKenzie in 1882 at Cape Juby (nowadays Tarfaya). (János Besenyő collection)

Mosque built by Ma El Ajnin in Smara. (János Besenyő collection)

were already heading towards Mauritania. Ma el Ainin was infuriated and gathered a large number of followers to help in his struggle. He started to fight against the French forces in 1895, and he went to Saguia el-Hamra where he founded the city of Smara.[26] He continued his attacks against the French forces in the 1900s, and in 1907, he asked the Moroccan ruler to assist him in his fight. In 1908, the campaign continued, and Ma el Ainin and his followers achieved some success. However, the Moroccan ruler turned against Ma el Ainin, and made a pact with the French. After announcing himself Mahdi, or the 'blue sultan', Ma el Ainin died in 1910, and his son, El Heiba continued the fight against the infidels. Nevertheless, he received a serious blow when in 1913 Colonel Mouret literally demolished the city of Smara. In 1916, during the First World War, a German submarine tried to assist the 'blue sultan', but the Spanish prevented this. When El Heiba died in 1918, his relative, Merebbi Rebbu went on to fight the French until 1926. In 1929, another relative of Ma el Ainin, Mohammed al Mamun, started to represent the Sahrawis. He continued the struggle, and in 1931–1932 he achieved some victories against French forces. In 1934, the French finished regulating the Sahrawi tribes, so the Spanish could start to colonise de facto the continental areas of the later Western Sahara.[27]

The Wake of the Sahrawi Statehood and the Events of the Twentieth Century Until 1975

Before entering into the examination of the events that led to the Sahrawi resistance against the Spanish, it is important to address some of the issues concerning the conditions in the area. On the shores of North Africa, there were two enclaves which were controlled by Spain: Mellila and Ceuta, which had been the property of the European power since the fifteenth and sixteenth centuries. The areas Spain possessed besides these were Ifni – which had belonged to Spain since 1860 and is now in Morocco – and Spanish Southern Morocco, Villa Cisneros and La Guerra. With the Second World War, some changes appeared in the territory.[28] By 1946 the Spanish had organised an administrative unit called Spanish West Africa comprising most of these areas, with Laayoune which would become its capital, having been established in 1940. However, in 1958 this entity was disbanded, and Spanish Sahara and Ifni continued as the new provinces of the Francoist empire.[29]

In the area of Spanish Sahara, the nomads were again not satisfied with the turn of events, as the activity of the Spanish provoked anti-colonial sentiments. They did not hesitate to express their dissatisfaction, and in 1938, they started a revolt which was quickly subdued by the Spanish Legion and much of the territory was controlled by the infamous military organisation. Besides the Legion, there were other organisations created by the colonisers. The Legion were helped out by the indigenous *Policia Territoria*, and the *Troopas de Nomadas* comprised of indigenous Sahrawis mostly on camelback. These nomad troops would later – after the Spanish Civil War – receive other responsibilities as well – their most important task was to regulate the Sahrawian tribes who were not easily ruled over, and they had to cover the borderlines to repulse incoming attacks. The Spanish Civil War was far away from the area, so it did not impact very much upon the life of the Sahrawis except that some joined Franco's army, and in 1937, some communists escaped the Villa Cisneros prison to disappear from the desert lands. At this time Laayoune became the centre of the administrative region, where there were only minor towns or rather villages and only a few people lived. The Second World War brought about some political turmoil because Hitler wanted to make use of the Saharan areas – as the Franco regime was an ally to him – and saw the area as a place of strategic value for his military plans. As mentioned, in 1946 Spanish West Africa was created. This brought about resistance from the Sahrawi tribes, which culminated in the renewal of the military actions of the indigenous people.[30]

The history of Western Sahara (then Spanish Sahara) continues with another uprising, which started in the mountains of the Rif and the Atlas. The Army of Liberation (or *Jaish at-Tahrir*) began its existence in 1955, when the Moroccan rural people rose against the exile of Mohammed V to Madagascar. The ruler would however soon return, and the independence of the country was no longer merely a dream for the people longing for freedom. In March 1956, Morocco finally became a sovereign state largely due to the persistent struggle of the Moroccan freedom fighters. Franco relinquished the so-called Spanish Southern Morocco in 1958 to the Moroccans, however he held on to the areas of today's Western Sahara, because he needed their vast phosphate sources and the abundant fishing industry.[31] After the stabilisation of the situation, nevertheless, Mohammed V wanted to pacify the rebels and he used them to supplement his Royal Army, the FAR (*Forces Armées Royales*) in order to bring the rebels under his control. Most of them joined, however the ever-renegade southern Sahrawi areas would not abandon fighting. Some of the southern Moroccan rebels went to the Spanish Sahara and called upon the warrior spirit of the Sahrawis to join the struggle on their side. They formed paramilitary units and stared to attack French garrisons and towns like Tindouf and Oum el-Achar in 1957, and even the Mauritanian French forces. Of course, this could have been a disaster for the French since they owned a large part of the Mauritanian iron ore-processor company MIFERMA (*The Societe Anonyme des Mines de Fer de Mauritanie*). In Ifni another revolt broke out against the Spanish colonisers. The impact of the rebels was so huge, and the Spanish had to retreat to the coastal areas of Western Sahara.[32] The French were infuriated, and together with the Spanish they planned an action against the rebels, which they named Operation Ouragan.[33] The rebels continued their actions, as they abducted some Spanish workers at Cape Bojador in November, and they closed in on El-Ayoun (the renamed Laayoune). The Europeans decided that it was time to launch their counter-invasion. The plan was to attack in two directions, the first in the direction of Smara, and the other to the south, to Río de Oro. The Spanish commander was Lieutenant General López Valencia and the French one was General Bourgund. The action began on 10 February 1958 and soon they drove out the guerrillas from the interior of the country. After this decisive victory, one further action occurred in March 1961, when guerrillas abducted several foreign workers, however, they were subsequently returned. This was to be the end of a decade-long-struggle, before fighting resumed in the 1970s.[34]

After the vicious fighting that occurred in the Saharan lands, a relatively peaceful era began. From the 1960s, the Sahrawis became more sedentary as the Spanish administration had introduced a series of developments into the country. Not long after the kidnapping of the oil workers in 1961, the Saharan people started to develop a certain national consciousness and began to establish their own organisations. The newly educated class of Sahrawis produced several intellectuals among whom one individual stood out: Mohamed Sidi Ibrahim Bassiri. He was born in Tan-Tan, received higher education in Casablanca, and went to Damascus and Cairo to learn more and discover the world. It is said that he became a Baathist, and he was a keen supporter of the pan-Arabist thesis. When he returned, he went to Spanish Sahara and in 1967, he established the organisation *Harakat Tahrir Saguia el-Hamra wa Oued ed-Dahab*, which became one of the first Sahrawi independence organisations in the region. However, the group had no intention of inciting revolt, and wanted to achieve their goals peacefully. This was nevertheless due to fail, since in one of their first actions, in 1970, they ignited the fire. Demonstrations were started to drive out the colonisers, however, the Spanish authorities responded with a clampdown, and many Sahrawis died. Their leader, Bassiri was presumed dead in the fighting, and so their movement suffered a setback.[35]

In examining the origins of the Sahrawi uprisings, it may be interesting to take a look at the organisations that developed in Morocco and were not originally Saharan by their nature, but showed the opposition of the people to colonisation, and in favour of independence. Eduard Moha – as he was called by his compatriots as an alias – was the initiator of MOREHOB (*Movement de Résistance des Hommes Bleues*) established in 1971. Besides instigating propaganda and some peaceful activities, they were mostly an insignificant group. In 1972, fighting broke out again, as some Sahrawis organised demonstrations against the Spanish in El-Ayoun and elsewhere. The result was several casualties on both sides. Another organisation, the 'Movement of 21 August' showed itself as well, but it was mainly constituted of Moroccans, and they followed the Moroccan cause.[36]

To understand better why Sahrawi nationalism developed so extensively and to comprehend the later fate of Western (Spanish) Sahara and the imperial thinking of the Moroccan empire, it is important to go back in time a little to examine the so-called Greater Morocco theory, because this idea served as one of the bases for Morocco to claim for itself the territories of the Sahrawi lands. In June 1956, the president of the Istiqlal (independence) party, Allal el-Fassi advanced an idea that was discarded at the time by the Moroccan ruler, but he later found it very interesting: however, it was so far-fetched that it could not be fully implemented. The nationalist Fassi stated that Morocco was the heir to the old Almoravid empire and thus had the inalienable right to claim several parts of the neighbouring countries, including territories from Spanish Sahara, Algeria, Mauritania and even some parts of Mali. As Mohammed V discovered, the idea that was considered exaggerated at first, was to soon become attractive, and with this, he sought to stabilise his rule in the newly independent country. Thus, in 1958 at the oasis of M'hamid he laid claim to the Saharan lands.[37] This was one of the bases for the Moroccans for the long process of demanding the rights to the Sahrawi areas.

After the tragic events of the 1972 clashes, and seeing the Moroccan claims to their lands, the Sahrawis had no choice but to resort to their old guerrilla tactics and took up arms again after the peaceful cohabitation with the Spanish. In 1973, a new organisation was created, which was to be decisive in the struggle of the Saharan people for their homeland. The so-called POLISARIO (or *Frente Popular para la Liberación de Saguia el Hamra y Río de Oro*) was founded by El-Ouali Mustapha Sayed, and the organisation began to harass Spanish outposts and settlements. For a start, they attacked the Spanish military base at El-Khanga on 20 May. They began an overwhelming offensive and looted several settlements and military outposts on their way. However, their most important victory was that they damaged the phosphate mines at Bou Craa and they destroyed the belt that transported the precious mineral to the port at Laayone, and thus they dealt a serious blow to the Spanish phosphate industry. In response, the Spanish tried to consolidate, and they created PUNS (*Partido del Unidad Nacional Sahrui*/ Saharan National Unity Party) in 1974 which was to represent the Sahrawi people in politics but was mainly composed of impressible elder sheikhs.[38] However, none of these happenings were enough to stop the events that led to the important year of 1975 in the conflict.

The UN had been eager to intervene in the conflict diplomatically and wanted to promote the cause of the rights of the Sahrawis. The first sign of the decolonisation movement that appeared in the UN was UN Resolution 1514 (XV) in 1960. This was the first statement in favour of the independence of the colonised countries and was followed by several resolutions that intended to move forward the case of the countries that were still in a state of oppression.[39] In 1961, the UN created a Decolonisation Committee (Special Committee on Decolonization or C-24), which started to take into consideration the rights of the Western Saharan people from 1963. The question of autonomy for the Sahrawis was brought forth by the UN several times during 1967–1973, and the issue became an important factor in the international political arena. In response to the demands of the UN, the Spanish started to organise for the possibility of an autonomous system and held a census to count the Sahrawis living in the area in 1974, with the resulting number being 73,497. All impediments had been removed from holding a referendum, which could have decided the fate of the territory.[40] At the peak of this

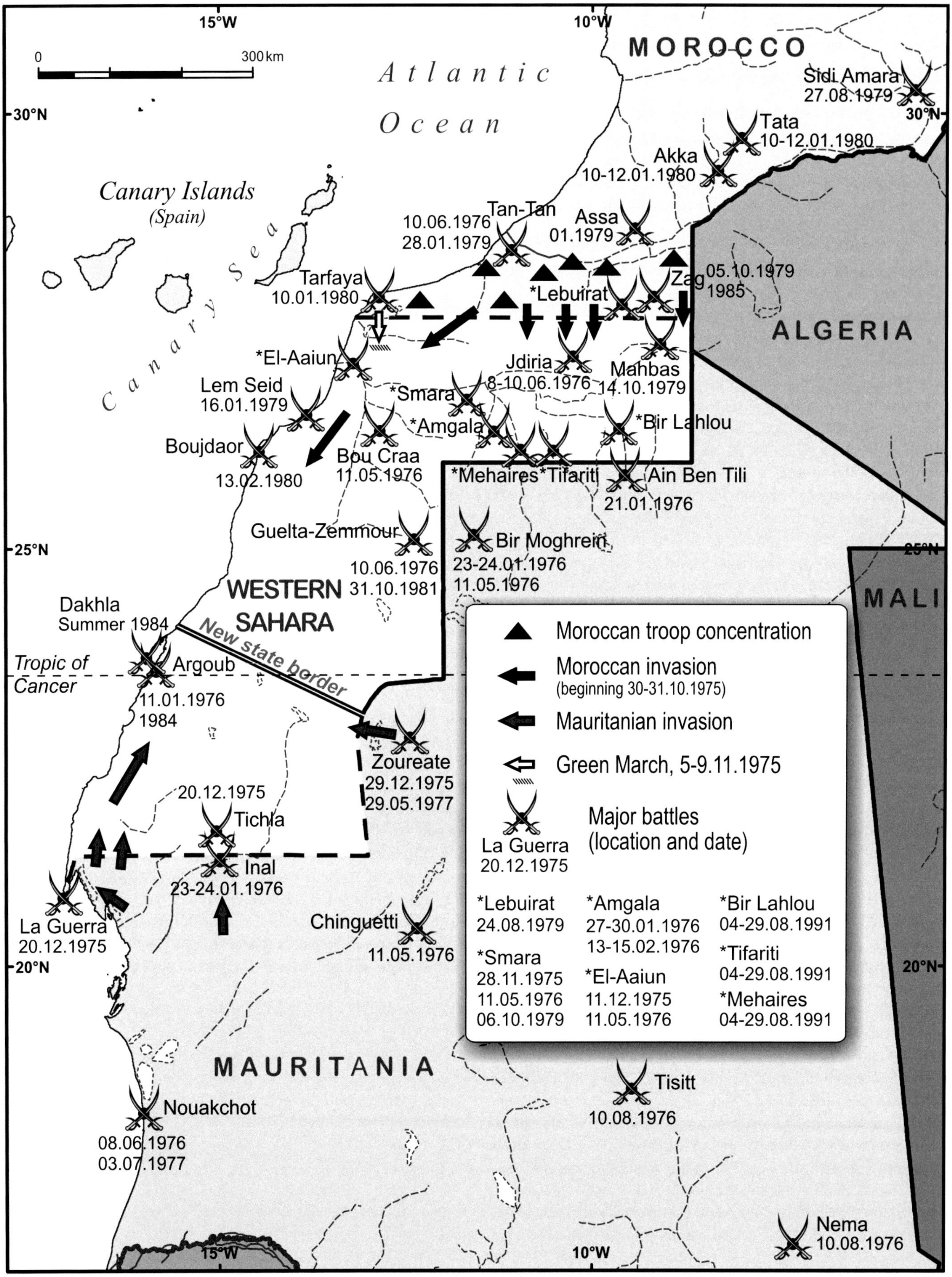

A map showing major events in Western Sahara. (Map by the author)

international effort to conduct a referendum in Western Sahara, the UN decided to publish Resolution 3292 (XXIX), which declared that the UN should send an investigative team to the area and to the neighbouring countries to be able to create an opinion on the rightfulness of a future vote.

The different countries had their own expectations of the visit. Morocco interpreted their claims on the basis that they levied taxes on the tribes in the given area, and the leaders of these groups of people had signed agreements with the Moroccan ruler. The Mauritanian opinion did not differ very much from that of the Moroccans, as they claimed that they have a common ancestry with the Sahrawis, which they associated with the ancient town of Chinguetti as the collective point of the tribes common to Western Sahara and Mauritania. Algeria voted, of course, for the autonomy of Western Sahara, as they decided that it was in their best interest to take this position. Spain's contribution to the talks was simple: Morocco and the other countries did not exercise formal rights over the mentioned areas in Western Sahara, so they had no right to claim any territory inside that land. After the committee with members from Ivory Coast, Cuba and Iran, arrived at the territory there was an official welcome parade organised by the Spanish and the pro-Spanish banners were highly visible, however, on the return trip the observers saw Polisario flags. The next leg of the trip was to Morocco, where the committee members visited Tan-Tan and Zag, where the delegates, of course, witnessed pro-Moroccan slogans and demonstrations. In Algeria they went to Tindouf, which had in recent years become the Polisario headquarters, and there saw that the people wanted sovereignty and autonomy for the area.[41]

When the decision in favour of autonomy was made final, Hassan II of Morocco did not waste any time, and made public his decision to organise a monumental demonstration into the area of Western Sahara, and he forecast that 350,000 people would take part in the event which he named the Green March. The Spanish manned their positions and prepared for the inevitable. On 6 November, the mostly civilian Moroccan procession entered Western Sahara and moved further into the interior. After long negotiations, the Moroccans were victorious and on 9 November, they withdrew their forces from the disputed lands. It had proven to be an effective policy by the king to solve his domestic political differences and to help him mend his differences with the military in his country. The final decision on the fate of the Saharan lands was made on 11 November 1975, when the so-called Madrid Accords were born. With the participation of Morocco, Mauritania and Spain, the parties agreed upon the sharing of the territories of Western Sahara: Morocco getting the northern part, while Mauritania got the southern one. The Spanish quit from the dispute, and decided they would soon leave. After the Spanish withdrawal – under the name Plan Golondrina – the Moroccans and the Mauritanians began to flow into the areas allocated to them.[42]

The Sahrawis were on the move at once, they were not going to give up their homeland without a fight, and so continued their guerrilla-style warfare. Of the two occupying countries, Mauritania was easier to attack, since its military forces were not as strong as those of the Moroccan army. The Sahrawis noticed this, and they started attacking Mauritanian settlements and military posts. and even reached Noukchott, the Mauritanian capital, with their leader El-Ouali at their side. They caused serious damage to the town, but they had to flee after the attack. Unfortunately for them El-Ouali died during the action. Just as before against Morocco, they dealt several blows to Mauritanian industry as well: they damaged the railway lines near the Zouerate iron mines, which were the principal economic resource of the Mauritanian government. They attacked again in 1976 and 1977, when they ruined one of the trains on the railway. The Sahrawi guerrillas attacked Noukchott again, this time with less success; however, it was a major blow for the Mauritanian government that their capital could be exposed to the desert people's attacks. France therefore intervened and tried to help the Mauritanians with a mission named Operation Lamantin, though with limited success, and later the Mauritanian government suffered serious consequences from this failure.[43]

After forcing the Mauritanians to withdraw in 1978, the Polisario Front could now concentrate its powers against its northern and more serious enemy, Morocco. They named their action as Operation Boumedienne, in honour of the Algerian president, and started to attack the Moroccan-occupied areas. In 1979 they attacked a town near Laayoune, then in the same year they went on to raid Tan-Tan. In the meantime, the Moroccans occupied the areas that Mauritania had been driven from. The Polisario Front started to recapture or at least harass the outposts of the Moroccan army in the interior of the desert country and at the end of the year, in October, they even reached Smara and they continued their offensive against the Moroccans.[44] In the beginning of 1980, they attacked towns near the Anti-Atlas, well inside southern Moroccan territory. The peak of their raids was however the assault against the oasis M'hamid, where Mohamed V declared that the Sahrawi lands were the property of the Moroccans. Their responses were several operations, named Ohoud, Zellagha and Iman. Under the leadership of the notorious General Ahmed Dlimi, the Moroccans slowly and painfully repulsed the Sahrawi forces. The largest innovation of the general was however the building of a wall system (called Hassan's Wall or Berm),[45] which shielded the economically important part of Morocco from the guerrillas, thus in 1982, the phosphate mining could restart.[46] Meanwhile, important things were happening in the Organization of African Unity (OAU), which acknowledged the Sahara Arab Democratic Republic in the same year; Morocco's response was instantly to quit the organisation, triggering political debates.[47] The wall – which was in the meantime expanded – was completed in 1987, and the areas important to Morocco in Western Sahara could be better defended from the attacks of the Sahrawi guerrillas.[48] Following a long diplomatic processes, the UN published Resolution 158/90 besides 160/90 which included the instructions for a future referendum. Finally, in 1991, the UN decided to establish a peacekeeping force that would supervise the implementation of the referendum and compliance with other decisions. The UN named the mission MINURSO (*Mission des Nations Unies pour l'Organization d'un Referendum au Sahara Occidental*).[49]

2
The Establishment of MINURSO: The Decisions Leading to the Peacekeeping Mission

The conflict in Western Sahara had already received serious international attention in the mid-1980s, so much so that UN Secretary-General Javier Pérez de Cuellar attended one of the OAU's key talks in 1985, during which he tried to negotiate a meeting between Morocco and the Polisario Front. The complexity of the situation was caused by the differing positions of the parties, as the Polisario Front wanted to negotiate with Morocco, which, in turn, refused to recognise the Western Saharan resistance movement. The positions of the parties eventually converged, and further consultations took place in New York during April–May. The negotiations eventually failed due to Morocco's stubborn resistance and refusal to make any concessions, so another attempt followed later. Saudi ruler King Fahd sat Moroccan and Algerian parties at the table, expressing their willingness to have an UN-led investigatory mission sent to the region.[1] The delegation arrived in the area at the end of 1987. As a result of their investigation, they prepared a draft titled 'Proposals of the Settlement of the Question of the Western Sahara' and signed by Isa Diallo, the Secretary-General's envoy. As the parties continued to express their displeasure with the planned proposals, in the summer of 1988 the Saudi leader once again mediated between the parties in the dispute and further negotiations took place, which were, however, unsuccessful. The elaborated settlement plan was still debated at length, and was finally submitted to the United Nations, where it was registered by the UN as Decree No. 621. To facilitate the implementation of the document, the Task Force for Western Sahara was established in June 1989, led by Special Envoy Isa Diallo, to enforce the terms of the agreement.[2] The draft included the following points:

- role and responsibilities of the UN leader in the mission
- controlling the ceasefire
- limitation of the presence of the Moroccan army
- a choice between two options during the referendum (independence or integration)
- verification of the legality of the vote by the United Nations
- settling the case of political prisoners
- the repatriation of Western Saharan emigrants

Remains of a BTR-60PB armoured personnel carrier destroyed in the 1991 clashes near Mehaires. (János Besenyő collection)

A T-54 main battle tank destroyed in the 1991 clashes near Tifarity. (János Besenyő collection)

MINURSO headquarters in El-Ayoun. (János Besenyő collection)

ceasefire, which entered into force upon the declaration of the Resolution.[4]

In August 1991, Morocco launched an attack on the Polisario forces and Moroccan troops penetrated deep into Sahrawian-controlled territory. The Sahrawis suffered significant losses and lost much of their heavy armament.[5] To avoid further atrocities between the parties and reaffirming the validity of the ceasefire – the UN decided to take decisive action, sending first 100,[6] and then 228 peacekeepers to the area to monitor compliance.[7] MINURSO need to be capable in the following areas:

- enforcement of the ceasefire
- adequate settlement of the situation of political prisoners
- conducting prisoner exchanges
- the implementation of a resettlement programme to repatriate alienated Sahrawis
- conducting the identification required for the referendum
- the proper, lawful conduct of the referendum and the announcement of the result[8]
- immediate publication of the result of the referendum and its enforcement within 24 weeks

After the UN gave its approval for the settlement plan, another visit of the Secretary-General to the countries concerned took place in 1990. From 29 July to 12 August, another inspection team arrived in the area.[3] The delegates sought to view the relationship between both parties, the legitimacy of their territorial claims, and the situation of refugees. The proposals made during the visits were incorporated into a UN Resolution, as a result of which, by Resolution 690 of 29 April 1991, the peacekeeping mission called MINURSO (*Mission des Nations Unies pour l'Organization d'un Referendum au Sahara Occidental*) was set up to monitor compliance with the ceasefire, which entered into force upon the declaration of the Resolution.

First, three sectors were created, in which 10 camps were established. The northern sector was commanded by a French colonel, the southern by a Chinese colonel, while the central sector was commanded by a Russian colonel.[9] This changed very quickly, as the central sector was abolished and the Russians took over the Tindoufi Liaison Office.[10]

North Sector headquarters in Smara. (János Besenyő collection)

The headquarters of the mission was set up in Laayoune, from where the organisation was coordinated. To this end, two sub-units were set up in Dakhla and Smara to accommodate a regional group headquarters in the south and one in the north. The third major administrative unit was set up in Tindouf, where a liaison office was set up to facilitate communication. This sector system worked until 2005, when all team sites came under the command of the mission, and the sector headquarters were abolished.[11]

The first peacekeepers to arrive began their work under very spartan conditions and without adequate logistical support from the United Nations. Australian Lieutenant

South Sector headquarters in Dakhla. (János Besenyő collection)

Liaison office in Tindouf. (János Besenyő collection)

Colonel Ian Campbell Gordon, who was the first to arrive on the mission, stated:

> The UN had none of its own equipment; no vehicles or radios, no food or water, no accommodation. Everything was on loan from the Moroccans and Polisario Front. The Australians in Laayoune were given two very sad looking Moroccan Army HF radio sets. They took the radios into a bedroom, cleaned off a table, strung an antenna on the roof and declared the Force Headquarters Radio Room open. The Radio Sergeant, Sergeant Paul Goodrick, and one of his Line Corporals arrived in Smara, 220 km to the east, and, with a single radio frequency at their disposal, they opened communications. A few days later, another two Australian soldiers were sent south to Awsard, about 600 km away, to open another sector headquarters. From the Force Headquarters in Laayoune, the Australians developed a single channel command radio net, taking on the sector headquarters and the UN observer team sites as they opened up. The Force Commander made very strong representation to have an extra 100 observers and the remainder of the Australian Signals Unit deployed, and the Australian contingent main body arrived in Laayoune on the night of 19 September. Next day, the Australians pushed forward to each of the 10 UN Team Sites, one at each team site with a full radio shift at each sector headquarters and at the Force Headquarters in Laayoune. Their job was to keep the Moroccan radios going and to train the observers in radio procedures.[12]

The American peacekeepers made a similar statement, and also criticised the accommodation and service conditions on the mission. Due to the lack of proper hygiene, several people got infections or fell ill, and four peacekeepers were evacuated in a serious condition.[13]

The peacekeepers were not only affected by dissatisfaction with the logistics supply, including food, water, and equipment, but also by the extreme weather conditions and inadequate accommodation.[14] The delivery of peacekeepers and logistics supplies was also a problem. At that time, the mission had two Antonov An-26 aircraft, four Mil Mi-8 helicopters and one Yakovlev Yak-40 aircraft. The An-26s were flown by Romanian pilots, the Mi-8 helicopters by Russians, while the Yak-40s were flown by Czechs. Although the machines and crews struggled with many shortcomings, their activities were successfully carried out.[15] Later, only Russian and Ukrainian pilots flew the aircraft.[16]

It was also a problem that a good number of military observers could not communicate in English, which made cooperation

One of the mission's An-26 aircraft landing in Oum Dreyga team site in 2007. (János Besenyő collection)

between peacekeepers significantly more difficult.[17] Despite all this, the military observers successfully carried out the tasks assigned to them, began patrolling and verified compliance with the ceasefire agreement. A particular problem was that Morocco had repeatedly blocked the handover of vehicles and other assets, such as ablution units and kitchen equipment, sent by the UN to the mission, which thus reached the peacekeepers several months late.[18] The peacekeepers, who arrived on 6 September 1991, could only take over their radios and vehicles in November, and until then they worked with equipment 'borrowed' from opposing parties.[19] According to American Lieutenant Colonel William C. Spracher, who served in the mission in 1992, Morocco only reluctantly allowed the peacekeepers in, hoping that they would legitimise the occupation of Western Sahara. When this did not happen, the Moroccans' willingness to cooperate with the UN decreased significantly. Moreover, according to the author, MINURSO employees were eavesdropped upon and observed, and their work was hindered.[20] In an article published in 2012, Spracher clearly stated that: 'Morocco was waging an active intelligence and counterintelligence campaign itself against the UN.'[21] The Moroccan secret service even did not allow the UN employees coming to the mission to enter the operation area but forced them to go to Rabat. Joseph Alfred Grinblat, a staff member of the Identification Office, wrote about this in his memoirs:

> We boarded a Royal Air Maroc plane in New York City, on Sept. 7, with 100 kilograms of luggage each, enough for an expected six months in the desert. When we arrived in Casablanca, on the morning of Sept. 8, however, we were not allowed to proceed to Laayoune and were taken by force to Rabat, the capital, by the Moroccan secret police. We were kept there for nearly two weeks, until Sept. 21, for what amounted to daily brainwashing sessions with people justifying Moroccan possession of Western Sahara. We found out that our abduction had been organized by the minister of interior of Morocco, Driss Basri, with the agreement of Zia Rizvi, who was waiting for us in Rabat.[22]

Several other reports mentioned the difficulties of cooperation with the Moroccan side too.[23]

Compared to Morocco, the Polisario Front seemed much more cooperative. According to Lieutenant Colonel Spracher, this was due to the fact that the Saharawis realised that they could not win independence through armed struggle, but the referendum guaranteed by the UN gave them a chance.[24]

Later, accommodation conditions and logistics for peacekeepers also improved significantly.[25] Nevertheless, the logistics system was not able to fully serve the mission and the peacekeepers serving in it because of the non-arrival of the Polish logistics battalion offered to the mission and no other logistics supply unit had been set up for the military contingent. Therefore, the military observers in the camps did not spend much of their time on patrols and other military tasks, but on logistical activities.[26] Unfortunately, this practice has survived to this day.[27]

The military observers serving on the mission also criticised the bureaucratic system of the UN for not providing adequate political support for MINURSO, and that adequate tools were not provided for peacekeeping activities. Therefore, the peacekeepers were only able to carry out their tasks to a limited extent.[28]

Tensions, however, did not diminish with the establishment of the peacekeeping mission. Partly because Morocco tried to turn the mission to its advantage, and if that did not work then to block it,[29] and the Moroccan side was still able to deploy its nationals on more favourable terms in order to influence the outcome of the referendum at a later date. The Polisario Front, of course, protested, as, for them, it was the indigenous Saharan population that was relevant to the outcome of the referendum, so they considered the population of the 1974 Spanish census to be the benchmark.[30] Morocco, on the other hand, wanted to add 120,000 people to the list who had not originally been included in the Spanish census. Of course, this was unacceptable to the Polisario Front, so, in the end, only 10,000 people were recognised as an addition by MINURSO's identification officials.[31] The expansion of the number of eligible participants was so important to the Moroccans that the leadership of the North African country even considered the prospect of another Green March if their demands were not met.[32]

All this resulted in the referendum originally scheduled for 1992 not taking place because the parties could not agree on fundamental

A Mil Mi-8 helicopter arrives at the Mijek team site with the weekly supply in 2008. (János Besenyő collection)

issues.[33] At that time, a change took place at the head of the UN, and Boutros Boutros-Ghali, a diplomat of Egyptian descent, became the Secretary-General. As the Sahrawi party did not consider Boutros-Ghali credible due to his previous views, as he had supported Morocco's position in the OAU before his appointment, it was difficult to achieve any rapprochement between the two parties. Finally, he submitted a draft proposing three possible solutions:

- the resumption of negotiations – this seemed rather hopeless
- the launch of the original settlement plan, taking into account the amendments made by Pérez de Cuellar, or
- elaboration of a new draft different from the previous ones[34]

As expected, the suggestions of the former Egyptian foreign minister did not resonate with the natives, so Boutros-Ghali had to find another solution. He visited the area in the spring of 1993 and then proposed five conditions under which a referendum could be held. As per them, the persons entitled to vote in the referendum would have counted who:

- participated in the 1974 referendum
- lived on the spot but whom the Spaniards left out from the list
- were relatives of the above persons
- were people with Sahrawi ancestors in Western Sahara
- and those who had lived in the area for six years continuously or 12 years intermittently before 1 December 1974

Although these conditions were still not entirely satisfactory to the parties, the system of conditions already seemed much more acceptable, even to the previously resisting Polisario Front.[35]

Beginning in 1993, US influence in the organisation was greatly strengthened as the United States began to play a more prominent role in leading the mission. Several results were achieved in the negotiations, such as improving the situation of Sahrawi prisoners, and this greatly helped bring positions closer together in the conflict.[36] Thanks to favourable conditions, the identification process was launched in August 1994, though it was often hampered by the parties' obstructive behaviour due to their different interests and points of view.[37] Morocco still submitted 180,000 applications at the last minute, resulting in 233,487 people being registered in the final aggregation. The inconsistent positions continued to cause tensions and disputes resumed from 1995 onwards, and, by 1996, the work of the Identification Office was rendered completely impossible, forcing it to suspend its activities temporarily.[38] Secretary-General Boutros-Ghali considered the situation so problematic that he did not consider it possible to continue the mission and called for its termination. The drastic solution was ultimately not accepted by the UN leadership, and the newly elected Secretary-General, Kofi Annan, was tasked with restoring confidence in the mission and relaunching it.[39]

This marked a turning point in the conflict and the mission. After so far largely unsuccessful mediation, the parties managed to reach an agreement in Houston, USA, in September 1997: the Houston Agreement was signed, returning to the principles of the original 1991 settlement, and thus bringing the parties somewhat closer together again.[40] This was preceded by an event previously considered unthinkable: direct talks between the opposing parties began in Lisbon on 23 June 1997, marking a turning point in the history of diplomatic relations. Thanks to all this, the mission continued its work, and in the summer of 1999, the staff of the Identification Office started the registration of the remaining three tribes of undetermined origin.[41] As a result, there were quite a few more, namely 147,249 new eligible voters registered, but only 86,381 of them passed the last filter, taking all conditions into account. However, not many of the members of the latest tribes surveyed – only 2,130 – were judged to be of an eligible background to vote.[42] As the outcome of the process created tension, there were sporadic uprisings in the affected municipalities in September 1999, but the Moroccan army quickly prevented further acts of violence. Surveying increasingly distant positions, Kofi Annan was forced to make another, more pessimistic estimate when he said the referendum could most likely take place in 2002.[43]

The next special envoy was the renowned American diplomat, James Baker, who also tried to settle the relationship, which was becoming increasingly tense due to resistance from the parties.

Sahrawi protesters in Laayounne in 2009 March. (János Besenyő collection)

In any case, it seemed clear that Morocco was ignoring the settlement plans and not complying with the Houston Agreement. Perhaps this was also due to the fact that the negotiating team led by James Baker resorted to a new-old solution when he travelled to the scene in April 2000, visiting all parties involved in the conflict. However, the series of negotiations ended again to no avail.[44] It seemed that the work of MINURSO would not be needed again for quite some time, and then another diplomatic scandal upset the mood. The Paris-Dakar Rally took place in January 2001, once again reviving territorial debates. The Polisario Front opposed the race as it would have passed through the regions controlled by the organisation and thus, in its interpretation, would have infringed its territorial integrity. Not much was needed, therefore, for the Sahrawis to take up arms again. Fortunately, the incident did not eventually escalate, and negotiations could continue in their original course. Baker did his best to smooth out the conflict and eventually drafted the Framework Agreement (also known as the Baker Plan) with his team.[45]

The innovation in Baker's offer was to grant the Sahrawi people within Morocco five years of partial autonomy. Specifically, this would have meant that foreign and military control would have remained in the hands of the Moroccans, but internal issues of governance would have remained in the hands of the desert people, so they could have a fairly strong influence over the area. After the five years, the referendum would have been held, for which Baker offered three options: complete freedom, autonomy, or full integration into Morocco.[46] Although Morocco considered the plan acceptable, the other side did not consider it appropriate and insisted instead on the old 1991 interpretation.[47]

The next step in the negotiations came soon after, as Algeria, Mauritania and the Polisario Front were invited to Pinedale, USA, where another series of talks began, but no agreement was reached on Baker's plan.[48] Then, an unexpected event that also strongly influenced the international public took place: on 11 September that year, a terrorist attack was carried out in the city of New York. Algeria was one of the first to respond to the incident, trying to provide assistance in everything to the United States. The Algerian president, Bouteflika, then, taking advantage of his sudden increase in influence, made an offer to Morocco to cut Western Sahara in two and divide it between Morocco and the Sahrawis, thus settling the decades-long dispute, but the Moroccan side did not accept the idea. It was not just Algeria's offer that gave a new direction to the negotiations, as the death of Hassan II, who was succeeded by Sidi Mohammed VI as king, also greatly influenced them. Initially, the international perception about the new king was good because, in many respects, he distanced himself from his father's previous politics and removed several politicians from their posts who opposed an agreement with the Polisario Front. However, those who expected him to take a new course in the question of Western Sahara would be disappointed. He continued to follow the same approach as his predecessor, and so negotiations kept stalling.[49]

Despite all this, more and more people within the UN wanted the operation to succeed and then be terminated, and despite French resistance, a refined version of the Baker Plan was accepted by the Security Council in 2003.[50] The new draft, prepared with the assistance of several internationally renowned experts, was completed by the end of 2002, then communicated to the parties with the approval of the Secretary-General, and finally published on 23 May 2003. About the new peace plan, Kofi Annan stated that it could satisfy both sides.[51] The new plan, while making concessions to both sides, favoured Morocco, according to independent political analysts and other experts. According to the final version, a referendum on the future of the area would have taken place in four to five years, during which time Western Sahara would have had wide-ranging autonomy in Morocco. An organisation – the Western Sahara Authority – would have been set up to prepare decisions in this area, administrate daily life and liaise with Moroccan official organisations. Its composition would be much more balanced than it could have been under the original plan where Moroccan refugees could have easily outnumbered the indigenous Sahrawis. During the transitional period, local finances, local taxes, education, fishing, security issues, and other matters affecting the life of the area would have been the responsibility of the organisation set up by the indigenous peoples, while the foreign affairs and defence sectors, including arms, except related to the armament of the Sahrawi law enforcement forces, would have remained under Rabat's control. This was a significant step forward from the previous agreement, as the legal system of Sahrawi autonomy would have been completely independent of Morocco and the repatriation of refugees to Western Sahara could have taken place. After the transition, a referendum would have been held that could have decided the fate of the area. Locals could have chosen between full independence, autonomy within Morocco, and full integration into Morocco. All persons over the age of 18 who were registered as permanent residents of Western Sahara since 1999 and who have been registered and qualified to vote by the United Nations as well as those living in refugee camps who were on the 'official list of residents to be resettled' created by the Asylum Office would have been eligible to vote. Although Morocco was unable to get its troops – approximately 120,000 – serving here to be eligible to vote, the result of the vote would have been very tight because of those who had settled here from Morocco.[52] Therefore, the Moroccan Ministry of Foreign Affairs sent a formal protest note to the Secretary-General criticising the Baker Plan and the role of the Algerian government in drafting the plan. However, in recent years, the Moroccan leadership had refined its position, supporting the draft insofar as it concerned only the issue of autonomy and not independence. While the Moroccan leadership did not respond, the Polisario Front shocked everyone by welcoming and accepting the new draft in its official statements.[53] Several experts explained the Sahrawi people's willingness to agree by the fact that the Sahrawis were exhausted, unable to continue the armed conflict, and a significant portion of the people and the leadership was tired of the fighting that had been going on for almost three decades. Seeing this, Morocco opted for a policy of waiting in the knowledge that it could not be forced to withdraw from the territories it occupied anyway. Between 2003 and 2005, the Polisario Front repeatedly indicated that it considered the refined version of the Baker Plan acceptable and that it would have been willing to start negotiations, but the Moroccan diplomats did not respond and waited. The tenacious diplomat Baker maintained his position for a while, but over time he had to realise that it would have been a pointless effort to continue to emphasise the same settlement principles, and, on 1 June 2004, he resigned and stopped his Western Saharan activities.

Due to the worsening security situation, several camps were fortified, surrounded with walls, and watchtowers were erected, from which it was easier to keep an eye on the surrounding area. This photograph shows the Mahbas team site fortification in 2010. (János Besenyő collection)

Baker's place was taken by John Bolton. Bolton wanted to hold the referendum, but soon realised that the Bush administration was in favour of autonomy within Morocco.[54] In addition, from 2005 onwards, an incident erupted in parallel with the Palestinian events, fundamentally affecting Western Saharan society, the outbreak of the so-called Sahrawi 'intifada', which began with efforts to free imprisoned Sahrawi political prisoners and then sparked sporadic protests.[55] Moroccan army forces responded to this with repression, which further heightened tensions. Then more and more uprisings took place in the area.[56] The expulsion of a Sahrawi activist, Aminatou Haidar, also caused tension, and in parallel with the Arab Spring, in October and November of 2010, Sahrawi protesters set up their centre called Gdeim Izik near the capital, from where they staged uprisings in the country. After the violent clashes, riots continued in 2011, which the Moroccan authorities had difficulty in quelling.[57]

In 2010, the UN renewed the mandate of MINURSO again, as violent incidents necessitated the continued presence of peacekeepers, even though they had already completed their census tasks.[58] In the following years, although the opposing parties took part in the 'mandatory' consultations, no positive change took place. As the UN was unable to make the parties change their positions, the situation that developed in prior years – 'neither peace nor war' – persisted.[59] There was a shift from this in 2018, when the US president appointed John Bolton as National Security Advisor and expected of him a solution to the Western Sahara issue as soon as possible. Using his past experience, the veteran US politician, pressuring the opposing parties at the UN, put them back at the negotiating table, but indicated that he would not tolerate the previously used time-consuming tactics as he set out to end the conflict in Western Sahara permanently. This, however, was not easy. In 2018, the UN Secretary-General's Special Envoy Horst Köhler visited several countries – Russia, the United States – and organisations – the African Union, the European Parliament – to seek their support for a permanent end to the conflict, and between 23 June and 1 July, he not only visited the mission, but surrounding countries as well, in part to find out the actual situation in person and to persuade the opposing parties to cooperate more. During the visit, it became clear that the ceasefire had been violated by the opposing parties several times, and that although MINURSO's security situation was very unstable and ineffective, the leaders of the opposing parties and surrounding states insisted on maintaining it. Although the opposing parties indicated that they wished to negotiate with each other, communication between them deteriorated and threats were exchanged on several occasions, which did not facilitate the negotiations.[60]

By 2018, MINURSO described the security situation as moderate, but considered the situation around Guergerat to be a source of tension. Although MINURSO considered the circumstances to be peaceful, it observed protests on several occasions during its patrols, which were usually organised by the Polisario Front and which were allegedly dispersed by Moroccans. Peacekeepers also experienced a number of drug-related activities against which they could not take action on their own. On 1 March 2018, MINURSO staff counted 225 personnel and patrolled the area under their supervision. They also sought to maintain control of Guergerat and to reduce and control conflicts between opposing parties.[61] Negotiations between the opposing parties took place again in Geneva from 5 to 6 December 2018, but no major progress was made, as Morocco continued to see only the limited autonomy offered in 2007 as any basis for negotiations, while the Polisario Front maintained that the Sahrawis vote on wanting an independent state or autonomy as part of Morocco as per the original peace draft. After that, it was decided to hold talks again in the first quarter of 2019.[62] The renewed roundtable negotiations took place on 21–22 March 2019, where, although a cooperative atmosphere was re-established, no agreement or progress was made, as neither side conceded its previous position. Despite this, it was agreed to continue negotiations.[63]

In 2019, MINURSO continued to operate in relatively calm conditions in Western Sahara. The ceasefire agreement and Military Agreement No. 1 were complied with by the parties. However, there was growing tension between the opposing parties in the Guergerat area. An unexpected event occurred on 22 May 2019 which made it difficult for the mission to function as Special Envoy Horst Köhler resigned from his position on medical grounds. On 31 August, MINURSO consisted of 236 personnel and guarded thousands of kilometres during patrols. He considered it an important task to maintain communications between Morocco and the Poisario Front and mediated on the contentious issues, in particular the issue of Guergerat. Unfortunately, the illegal drug trade and the growing activity of terrorist groups became an increased threat in the area, forcing the mission to take security measures.[64]

3
The Further Work of MINURSO – a Review of the Mission's Recent Developments

After the long, 30-year period of ceasefire and diplomatic stalemate, by the 2020s, the situation in Western Sahara began to change both regionally and internationally. After the previous, relatively peaceful period of truce, disagreements intensified and the animosity between the opposing parties strengthened, and as a result, the stability of the Western Sahara region began to become more and more unstable. Although the referendum that led to the creation of the mission has not yet been implemented, MINURSO remained on the ground and, with the help of its military and police personnel, continued to try to maintain the status quo.[1] In addition to ground and air patrols, the peacekeepers dealt with demining, as well as curbing the arms trade, the drug and human trafficking and other illegal activities in the region. Furthermore, special attention was paid to keep in touch with individual tribal leaders and leading politicians of the opposing parties, but this did not lead to an agreement on the fate of the area. By 2020, the situation had become increasingly worse, and due to the renewal of hostilities, even an armed conflict became probable, which indeed erupted at the end of 2020 due to the escalation of the Guerguerat conflict.

The Situation in Western Sahara Today

By the end of the 2010s, the fate of Western Sahara had still not been settled. Since the 1991 armistice, there had been no armed clashes between the opposing sides, yet the antagonism became more and more tense by the end of the decade. Both the Polisario Front and Morocco tried to do everything in order to improve their situation both regionally and internationally. The activities of MINURSO, which tried to facilitate the maintenance of peace, contributed greatly to the preservation of the status quo. Nevertheless, in 2016, tensions arose again between the organisation and Morocco, as the UN Secretary-General at the time, Ban Ki-moon, used the term 'occupied territory' in relation to Western Sahara. The Moroccan government protested and then expelled most of MINURSO's civilian employees from the country. Since they were responsible

An Mi-8 helicopter preparing for an air patrol in 2010. (János Besenyő collection)

The view from crew cabin as MINURSO peacekeepers conduct an air patrol. (János Besenyő collection)

Hungarian peacekeeper Major Kálmán Kalló on air patrol, Mijek 2009. (János Besenyő collection)

for the logistical supply and service of the mission, MINURSO found itself in a very difficult situation in certain areas. Although the soldiers took over several activities previously carried out by civilians, the operation of the mission became significantly more difficult. After several consultations, Morocco lifted the restrictive measures against the operation, but the mission continued to face difficulties. In March 2019, Horst Köhler, the UN Special Representative (Special Representative of the Secretary-General/SRSG), tried to bring the opposing parties to the negotiating table again. He organised a meeting in Geneva between Algeria, Morocco, Mauritania, and the Polisario Front.

The discussions were interpreted completely differently by the opposing parties. Both the Sahrawi organisation and Morocco emphasised that their positions prevailed during the discussions.[2] However, despite Köhler's efforts, the peace negotiations soon broke down, so in May 2019, Köhler resigned from his mandate, as a result of which Morocco tried to persuade as many states maintaining good relations with it as possible to operate consulates or other diplomatic or economic organisations within Western Sahara. In response, the Polisario Front organised a blockade of the highway located in the Guerguerat area near the Mauritanian border, then proceeded to occupy a part of it. As a result, motor vehicle traffic to Mauritania and Senegal was completely blocked and so Moroccan traders and transporters suffered a significant economic loss. Due to the situation, Moroccan army units appeared in the area, and on 13 November 2020, they began removing roadblocks and even used weapons against the Saharawi protesters. Militants of the Polisario Front intervened and rescued the demonstrators, after which the organisation cancelled the existing ceasefire and launched attacks against the Moroccan forces.[3] The renewal of hostilities ended a period of about 30 years of peace and sparked a limited armed conflict.

In such a situation, it was not easy for MINURSO, which since the mid-2000s has only dealt with the observance of the ceasefire provisions, the maintenance of the status quo, and performed tasks related to the security of the region. The development of the conflict was not only worrisome at the local level, but also seemed dangerous in terms of the regional area. In the region of North Africa, there had long been a cause for concern that terrorism and migration were manifesting themselves more and more on the ground, and the current problems related to Western Sahara could easily lead to the strengthening of radical Islamist groups and an increase in migration towards Europe. If the situation continued to escalate and more serious acts of war took place between the sides, it could even lead to the outbreak of a regional war.[4] That is why, in addition to local confrontations, it is worth examining the events of the wider region as well.

The Sub-Saharan region and North Africa together continue to be a hotbed of conflicts, which in the latter region mainly manifests itself in the tension affecting Western Sahara and the unresolved situation in Libya. Since the events of 2010, the situation in Libya has been unclear and there are still difficulties in maintaining order in a country ruled by warlords.[5] It is also a problem that the decades-long conflict between Morocco and Algeria, which has negatively affected the stability of the Maghreb region, was renewed again when Algeria decided to block gas shipments coming to Spain via Morocco. The main reason was the renewed conflict between the Polisario Front and Morocco, and since Algeria is known to support the Sahrawi organisation, the re-emergence of this regional conflict can be considered as a response to the worsening of the situation.[6] As a result of this and the outbreak of the conflict in Western Sahara, the stability of the region weakened, so illegal drug trade and gun running, as well as migration and terrorism, could be expected to increase in the desert area. The threat to the zone was thus likely to increase and the regional security risk of the local countries will become greater. Unfortunately, the relationship between Western Sahara and Morocco remains fragile, and the renewed conflict will continue to affect the security situation in the region.

However, events were given a completely new perspective by the fact that in December 2020, US President Donald Trump officially recognised Morocco's sovereignty over Western Sahara, which was considered an extremely great diplomatic success for the North African country. The recognition was in return for the country's recognition of Israel not long before. Due to a remarkable turn for the Middle East and the African region, the decades-long status quo was overturned, and this also caused the situation to escalate.

The regional situation worsened further when, in July 2021, the Moroccan ambassador to the UN, Omar Hilale, made a politically sensitive statement when he praised the independence aspirations of the Kabyle population seeking autonomy in Algeria. As a result, Algeria broke off diplomatic relations with Morocco, thus creating another source of tension in addition to the Western Sahara conflict. Meanwhile, new – albeit not very intense – clashes broke out in the disputed Western Sahara area, and in November, an Algerian truck convoy passed through the Sahrawi area, which the Algerian side said was hit by an enemy bomb attack. The Moroccan side did not claim responsibility for the attack. The renewed clashes were greatly influenced by the new Saharawi generation, which is less and less willing to acknowledge the established status quo and which expressed its anger in small attacks against the Moroccan army.[7] The conflict became more and more complex as a result of the new developments and maintaining and stabilising the security situation promised to be an increasing challenge for MINURSO. To facilitate this, in 2021, Staffan de Mistura was appointed as the UN's special envoy for issues affecting Western Sahara. The diplomat quickly got to work and tried to bring the opposing parties to the negotiating table again. On 12 January 2022, he started his activities by visiting the war zone, and on 15 January, he held talks with the leader of the Polisario Front, Brahim Ghali. But Mistura soon faced an escalation of tensions in the region, as Algeria then cut diplomatic ties with Morocco over the aforementioned comments on the Kabyles. In fact, he faced further difficulties, as on 19 March, Algeria also recalled its ambassador to Spain, as the Spanish sided with Morocco on the Western Sahara issue. However, as Polisario Front had refused to comply with the provisions of the ceasefire agreement in the area since November 2020, the UN and MINURSO will have to face additional difficulties.[8]

After outlining the security policy situation of the North African region, it is worth taking a look at the region's international, transcontinental relations. Russia, for example, has a strong influence on the area, influencing the region's political processes in many ways. In several countries of the Sahara region, Moscow still plays a decisive role. With regard to the conflict in Western Sahara, Russia traditionally claims a neutral position, as it does not want to upset the stability of the region, however, among the local states, it primarily has good relations with Algeria, since the Arab country obtains most of its weapons from it. From a geopolitical point of view, the North African states show a complex picture as a result of the competition between the great powers, as the events triggered by the Arab Spring further deepened the political antagonism between Russia and the West, especially the USA and France, the main source of which was the events in Syria in the 2010s.[9] In addition, Russia is increasingly trying to take a more active role in the dispute concerning Western Sahara; in October 2021, high-ranking Moscow diplomat Mikhail Bogdanov officially received Polisario Front representatives, thus breaking with the previous tradition that the organisation is not officially received in the country. Moscow's move is in all likelihood a consequence of Morocco's recognition of Israel, and therefore in return, a reinforcement of its claims to Western Sahara from the United States. It is therefore possible that the Russian state, by recognising the Polisario Front at such a high level, would like to counterbalance the American geopolitical dominance, so that it does not lose its existing influence in the region, or possibly even strengthen it.[10]

MINURSO's Role in the Western Sahara Conflict Since the Mid-2010s

MINURSO practically faced a new task from the 2000s, as the identification process was completed, and the referendum was prepared. Despite this, the referendum has not taken place to date. However, the organisation was still needed, as the security policy challenges did not disappear, and the international mission was needed to deal with them. By the mid-2010s, MINURSO gained more and more importance as a peacekeeping organisation due to regional influences – radicalism, drug and arms trafficking, migration, and local clashes – but had to intensify its efforts more and more in order to stabilise the situation in the region. This, however, was not easy due to the limited personnel and financial conditions at its disposal. The first major shock to the organisation came during the diplomatic tension created by Ban Ki-moon in 2016, when the UN Secretary-General claimed in a statement that Morocco had invaded Western Sahara. In response, Morocco expelled part of the MINURSO staff and imposed restrictions on the mission.[11] Not long after, one of MINURSO's main shortcomings was brought up, which was raised by Mozambican President Chiassano on 1 May: the mission's mandate does not include the issue of human rights, which could be problematic in terms of the organisation's activities in the region.[12] MINURSO struggled with additional mandate addition problems, as in 2018, its mandate was only extended by half a year instead of one year, although UN Secretary-General António Guterres would have recommended the latter.[13] MINURSO was also faced with the fact that the conflict in the Guergerat region had exacerbated the security policy situation in Western Sahara, so the peacekeepers had to respond to violations of the ceasefire regulations committed by the opposing sides in many more cases than before. True to its previous practice, MINURSO once again called for a peaceful solution to the situation and tried to reconcile the Moroccan and Saharawi parties, as far as it proved possible. Although MINURSO – as before – tried to promote a negotiated solution, all efforts proved futile.[14]

In the meantime, MINURSO faced not only security policy challenges, but also difficulties caused by the COVID-19 pandemic. In 2020, the pandemic not only caused logistical problems for the

Unexploded aerial bomb found in the Mehaires area. (János Besenyő collection)

Unexploded artillery shell near Bir Lahlou. (János Besenyő collection)

Anti-tank mine near Smara. (János Besenyő collection)

organisation, but also capacity reductions, as patrol activities could only be carried out with reduced numbers and intensity, so fewer weapons supervision activities took place in Western Sahara. In addition to the reduced presence, contact with the liaison office in Tindouf also became more difficult, and the peacekeepers were also faced with the fact that the opposing parties violated the ceasefire more and more often. By the middle of 2020, the level of rule violations had increased strongly, the individual data report a total of 61 rule violations, of which Polisario Front committed the largest number, a total of 53. MINURSO also faced other problems: the Moroccan forces started construction and fortification works along the Berm without permission. Furthermore, the illegal drug trade in the region increased, against which the peacekeepers were not able to act effectively. In addition to drug trafficking, illegal migration and human trafficking have also gained significant ground in recent years, so the mission had to pay attention to this as well when monitoring the area.[15]

The situation was further aggravated by the fact that Polisario Front continuously obstructed the free movement of MINURSO personnel and even restricted the movement of convoys providing logistical support for the peacekeepers. Therefore, after a while, the camps operating in the areas controlled by the Polisario Front could only be supplied by air, which made the logistical supply of the peacekeepers very difficult. As a result, the quality of the observers' food also deteriorated, as they did not have access to enough fresh supplies.[16] Another difficulty for MINURSO was that demining activities slowed down due to the conflict around Western Sahara, so mines and unexploded ordnance continue to pose a threat not only to peacekeepers, but also to the civilian population.[17]

2021 proceeded similarly compared to the previous years and the COVID-19 pandemic continued to complicate the situation of MINURSO. Although the peacekeepers tried to adapt to the situation, a military observer fell victim to the pandemic on 30 August. Despite this, patrolling continued, albeit on a limited basis. The COVID-19 pandemic also put Algeria, Morocco, and the Polisario Front in a difficult situation, yet each country's reaction to the pandemic was different. Due to its health situation, Algeria was only able to make modest preparations for the pandemic situation, which is why the North African country was highly affected by COVID-19. Algeria suffers from a lack of adequate infrastructure, so it started its treatment of the disease from a much more disadvantaged position. Morocco, on the other hand, is a richer and better-equipped country, so found it was somewhat easier to overcome the difficulties caused by the pandemic. The Liberated Zone and the Sahrawi refugee camps in Algeria also suffered from the pandemic, as the disease spread among the Saharawi population causing many problems as well.[18]

Unfortunately, the willingness of the opposing sides to cooperate deteriorated and they violated the provisions of the ceasefire agreement on more and more occasions, against which the peacekeepers were unable to act effectively. The free movement of peacekeepers was also restricted several times, so they could only carry out their duties to a limited extent. Likewise, the activities of terrorist organisations and other criminal activities (drug and human trafficking) increased in the region, which also posed a challenge to the patrols.[19] Due to the volatility of the security situation, the role of MINURSO has therefore become more important, which is why, despite various criticisms, its mandate was renewed again, based on Resolution 2602, until 31 October 2022.[20]

Finally, what is still very current in international politics and has had an impact on Africa and the Western Sahara issue as well, is the Russian-Ukrainian war. The conflict that started in early 2022 (and is ongoing at the time of writing) not only caused significant tensions in Europe, but also caused problems on the African continent. Several African politicians, such as Macky Sall, the president of the African Union, called on Russia to comply with international agreements and to stop aggression in Ukraine. One of the reasons he did this was because he was afraid that African separatist organisations would see it as an example of secessionist efforts, which would also negatively affect MINURSO. It is a serious challenge for the North African region that Ukraine and Russia are two of the main suppliers of grain to the region, so their absence creates additional security risks. One of the main geopolitical factors is gas and oil trade between the continents: an embargo on Russia may be good for North African states, but if Moscow sells gas to the east, African countries will have fewer options since China buys a lot of oil and gas from the continent.[21] In addition, the energy crisis has further implications for Africa, as inflation and the price of oil and grain began to rise sharply as a result of the war. Russia is also increasingly present militarily in the region and has already deployed one of its favourite mercenary armies – the Wagner Group – in many African countries for peacekeeping or other activities.[22] As a result of the difficulties, diplomatic activity in the region increased significantly, for example, US Secretary of State Anthony Blinken visited Algeria and Morocco in March 2022, where he assured Morocco of his support and tried to distance Russia from Algeria. Algerian President Abdelmajid Tebboune expressed his support for Russia, as the two nations have long had strong trade ties. The Algerian president continued to call on Morocco to resolve the situation in Western Sahara.[23] Another important link in the region's relationship to the war may be that Morocco did not vote for the statement issued by the UN condemning Russia, which is why the situation is becoming increasingly complicated. In addition, one of the international consequences of the Russian-Ukrainian war is that Russia is even more actively trying to realise its political interests in the region and is trying to influence the African gas supply to Europe through Algeria and Libya.[24] Western Sahara and MINURSO are also affected by this war in that the United States is turning with renewed interest to the fate of the area, since Russia's war gave Algeria an advantage, as the North African country decided to cut off its gas supply to Morocco and thus to Spain, thereby gaining a political advantage regarding Western Sahara.[25]

MINURSO peacekeepers reverted to tried and tested maps in the event of GPS failure. (János Besenyő collection)

Summary

Ultimately, it can therefore be stated that the political and social events of the 2020s in the North African region, above all in Western Sahara, changed the life of MINURSO, which was forced to adapt to the difficulties of recent years, the COVID-19 pandemic and the Russo-Ukrainian war. Life in Western Sahara was also made difficult by the latest developments, and the suppressed conflict between the opposing sides erupted again. Although MINURSO continues to try to fulfil its mandate, it has less and less influence on events in the area. Meanwhile, the international situation is constantly evolving, and it can be seen that great powers such as the United States, Russia, and China are doing everything they can to expand their influence. The shock caused by the Russo-Ukrainian war also reached North Africa's gas supply and grain deliveries, as on the one hand Algeria shut off the taps to gas reaching Spain via Morocco, thus strengthening its partnership with Russia, while at the same time events took place that shook the whole region, as the absence of Ukrainian and Russian grain imports has had an extremely negative effect on the food supply of the region, which therefore suffers from a shortage, and this increases the tension in the countries of the region. All in all, the 2020s have brought significant changes both in the life of the conflict in Western Sahara and in the development of the international situation, and crisis situations such as the COVID-19 pandemic and the Russo-Ukrainian war have greatly affected the stability of the North African region.

Hungarian peacekeeper Lieutenant Colonel Sándor Szomolányi on night patrol, Mahbas, 2010. (János Besenyő collection)

The Possible Fate of MINURSO

Although the peacekeeping mission present in Western Sahara since 1991 has not been able to carry out what it was created for – the referendum on the future of the territory – in recent years, it has performed such important tasks as the registration of those entitled to vote, patrolling activities, etcetera, which contributed to maintaining the stability of the region.

Although many have criticised the activities of MINURSO, it is indisputable that it has maintained a kind of status quo and the opposing parties tried to achieve results through negotiations and not armed struggle. However, the results achieved in the 1990s and at the turn of the millennium have less and less of an impact today. The events of the Arab Spring transformed not only the Middle East, but also the North African region, which did not leave Western Sahara untouched either. The conflict between Polisario Front and the Moroccan army, the COVID-19 pandemic, and the Russo-Ukrainian war, whose impact on the African continent experts do not even dare estimate, have affected the activities of the mission negatively. It is also a problem that various Muslim radical organisations and terrorist groups have been increasingly active in the region since 2010, and the activities of various criminal organisations (human and drug trafficking, gun running) are also increasing, which also pose an amplified risk to peacekeepers. The blockade near Guergeurat in 2019 exacerbated the tension between Morocco and Polisario Front – which represents the Sahrawis – which only intensified in the following years. In 2020, another important change occurred in the regional political situation, as the USA recognised Moroccan sovereignty over Western Sahara. This immediately provoked the resentment of Algeria, as a result of which the long-standing diplomatic antagonism between the two neighbouring countries was renewed again. The conflict that erupted again between the opposing sides in November 2020 further complicated the situation in the region, which is why it was increasingly difficult for MINURSO to carry out the activities included in its mandate. After the events of the past years, the mission is faced with more and more problems that make its work even more difficult, so it must make an increased effort to preserve peace in the region.

Regarding the future fate of MINURSO, it can be said that there will still be a great need for the operation of the organisation in the region, as the renewed armed conflict in Western Sahara and the situation between Algeria and Morocco have escalated and could potentially lead to a further deterioration of the security situation in the region, or even a regional war. So far, MINURSO has reliably performed the tasks assigned to it by its mandate, but this will probably not be sufficient in the near future. It would be necessary to expand the mandate of the mission to include the monitoring of humanitarian rights, to strengthen and expand the number of military, police, and civilian components, and to transform the mission's logistics system so that it better adapts to changing requirements. Although the possibility of abolishing the costly mission arises from time to time, this is not supported by the international community or the opposing parties, since MINURSO is the only international organisation capable of maintaining the status quo – if only to a limited extent. That is why MINURSO can assume an increasingly important role in maintaining the security of the region in the coming period. In addition to its previous tasks, the mission can increasingly focus on solving and handling security policy challenges. However, this will not be easy, as the war will probably drag on, the COVID-19 pandemic has still not abated, the activities of terrorist groups in the region are intensifying, and there is also illegal migration, all of which complicate the activities of peacekeepers. MINURSO's mandate has had to be extended every year, but this period may even be halved due to rapidly changing/deteriorating conditions. If the peacekeepers are not able to maintain the status quo, or if the conflict in Western Sahara continues to escalate, it could have a negative impact not only on the Maghreb region, but also on North Africa and even the Middle East. This is why China, Russia, and France are expected to increase their presence in the mission. Moreover, it is not inconceivable that the United States will also try to participate more actively in the mission, similarly to its role in 1993.

In summary, the role of MINURSO is expected to increase in the coming years, as the more active presence and activities of peacekeepers will become necessary in order to ensure the stability of the region.

4 The Structure of MINURSO

After a more detailed description of the history of Western Sahara and a brief history of MINURSO, the peacekeeping mission set up by the UN there, it is worth taking a look at the organisation's inner workings. A more comprehensive understanding of the mission is essential in order to understand its operation, function, and nature. MINURSO is the oldest continuously operating mission of the UN in Africa, which has become crucial in the disputed area and continues to play an important role in the region to this day. As mentioned in the previous chapter, in the beginning, in addition to law enforcement, the coordination of conducting the registration process was also one of its tasks. However, after this was completed in 2003, the mission now only fulfils the classical peacekeeping roles. In light of this, it is worth presenting its organisational structure in addition to its activities. The following chapter attempts to give an accurate picture of the internal structure of MINURSO operating in Western Sahara and the activities of those serving there.

MINURSO is subordinate to the Secretary-General of the United Nations (United Nations Secretary-General, UNSG), but his management rights are exercised by his Special Representative (Special Representative of the Secretary-General/SRSG), who is also the first leader of the mission. The military management of the mission is carried out by the military commander of the mission (Force Commander, FC) based on the request of the UN Secretary-General and upon the agreement of the Security Council. His work is supervised by the military advisor at the UN headquarters in New York, while simultaneously informing the special envoy of the Secretary-General. MINURSO is headquartered in the city of Laayoune situated in the centre of the Moroccan-occupied territories.[1] 245 military personnel and two police officers serve in the mission.[2] Of these, 218 people work as military observers, while another 27 people work in other positions serving and ensuring the coordination of the mission (a 20 strong Bangladeshi medical team and seven Ghanaian non-commissioned officers serving as

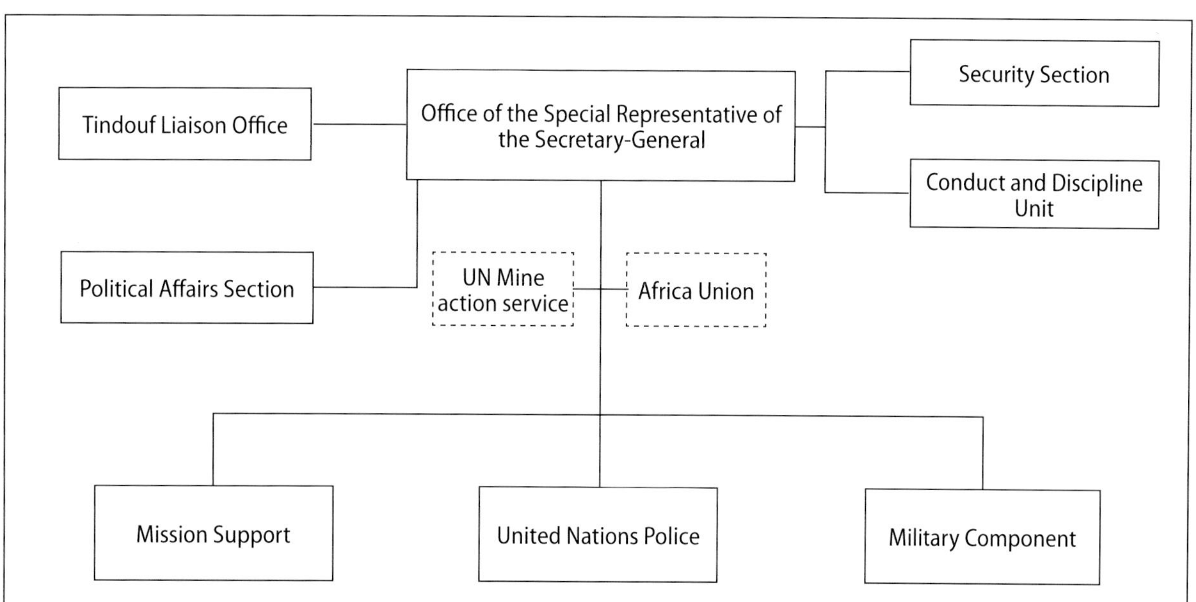

The structure of MINURSO. (Chart by author)

clerks).[3] The following states sent military observers and police officers to the mission: Argentina, Austria, Bangladesh, Belgium, Bhutan, Brazil, China, Croatia, Djibouti, Dominican Republic, Ecuador, Egypt, El Salvador, France, Germany, Ghana, Guinea, Honduras, Hungary, India, Indonesia, Italy, Japan, Jordan, Kazakhstan, Malawi, Malaya, Mexico, Mongolia, Nepal, Nigeria, Pakistan, Philippines, Poland, Portugal, Russia, South Korea, Sri Lanka, Sweden, Switzerland, and Togo.[4]

The civilian component of the mission currently consists of 248 people.[5] These include the office of the SRSG, the Security Section, the Conduct and Discipline Unit, the Political Affairs Section, the Tindouf Liaison Office, and the Mission Support. The departments of the organisation do not include the previously abolished Identification Office. The local office of the African Union, the UN Mine Action Service, and the local representatives of the UNHCR, who are primarily active in the refugee camps in Algeria, also do not belong to the mission, but cooperate closely with it. The remainder of this chapter describes the military components of MINURSO.

The Military Contingent

Initially, three sectors were created in the area of operation, in which 10 camps were established. The northern sector was commanded by a French colonel, the southern by a Chinese colonel, while the central sector was commanded by a Russian colonel.[6] This later changed as the central sector was abolished, and the Russians were given the leadership of the Tindouf Liaison Office as 'compensation.' The sectors were abolished altogether during the restructuring of the mission in 2005, and since then, the camps have been directly under the headquarters

Awsard team site in 2002. (János Besenyő collection)

Oum Dreyga team site in 2002. (János Besenyő collection)

Mahbas team site in 2003. (János Besenyő collection)

Agwanit team site in 2003. (János Besenyő collection)

Mijek team site in 2003. (János Besenyő collection)

Mehaires team site in 2003. (János Besenyő collection)

of the mission.[7] There are currently nine team sites. Four of them (Awsard, Oum Dreyga, Smara, and Mahbas) are west of the wall system in the area controlled by Morocco, while another five (Agwanit, Mijek, Mehaires, Tifariti, and Bir Lahlou) are east of the wall system, in the area controlled by the Polisario Front.[8] The officers who send soldiers to the mission and are suitable for military observation work – trained by the UN or the sending governments – serve in these camps. It is an unwritten rule of MINURSO that, if possible, two military observers belonging to the same nation only serve in the same camp in exceptional cases.[9] Of course, this can only be effectively applied to the soldiers of countries sending smaller contingents, though efforts are made to apply the same principle to those serving at the headquarters as well.

In addition to their own national regulations, the work of MINURSO officers is regulated by the mission's regulations and the military agreements concluded by the mission with the opposing sides. The first military agreement (Military Agreement 1) was concluded by the Royal Moroccan Army, Polisario Front, and MINURSO in December 1997 and January 1998. The agreement includes actions that violate the provisions of the ceasefire agreement and authorises peacekeepers to investigate them.[10] The purpose of the agreement is to maintain the status quo. Although the agreement was kept by the opposing parties, its provisions have been violated in several cases over the past years. The second agreement (Military Agreement 2) was concluded between MINURSO and the Polisario Front in April 1999, while the third agreement between the Royal Moroccan Army and MINURSO was concluded in March 1999.[11]

Tifariti team site in 2003. (János Besenyő collection)

Bir Lahlou team site in 2002. (János Besenyő collection)

The purpose of the agreements is to reduce the mine threat to the population, opposing parties as well as the peacekeepers, as the area is dotted by a large number of unexploded mines and artillery ordnance. In the past, the opposing parties did not always share with the peacekeepers the locations of the minefields they planted, and thus several incidents took place.[12] In 1992, in one such incident, the vehicle of the peacekeepers ran onto an anti-tank mine, which exploded. An American major and an Italian captain were seriously injured in the explosion.[13] In another incident, a car driven by a Peruvian peacekeeper ran over an anti-personnel mine. The driver of the vehicle got away with minor injuries from the explosion.[14]

Pursuant to the agreements, the peacekeepers mark the mines they discover and then hand over the exact coordinates to the opposing parties, who destroy them with the means at their disposal. Previously, only the Moroccans were able to carry out this activity, the Polisario Front – due to the lack of adequate equipment and training – less or not at all.[15] Since 2008, this activity has been coordinated and supervised by the United Nations Mine Action Service (UNMAS) in the area of the mission, in cooperation with the opposing parties.[16]

Those serving at the headquarters are – in general – divided according to the structure in force in the organisations of NATO. The duties of staff officers are regulated by the mission's regulations (Standard Operating Procedures for Peacekeeping Operations, SOP).

The main duties and obligations of the staff officers serving at the headquarters are:

- Preparing proposals for the commander and chief of staff on professional issues
- Cooperation with civic organisations, coordination and management of their professional work
- Cooperation with other military departments (G1 personnel, G3 operational service, G4 logistics service, etcetera)
- Professional preparation and supervision of those serving in the patrol camps and professionally subordinate to them
- Preparation of various reports for MINURSO and the New York headquarters
- Providing up-to-date information to the chief of staff on professional matters

The following departments operate at the headquarters of the mission:

Personnel Department

The duties of the department of personnel include the management of all personnel tasks concerning military observers belonging to the MINURSO staff (travel, duty trips, unexpected deaths, accidents, medical examinations or treatments, etcetera), preparation of military IDs, preparation of various reports and opinions thereof, assistance in matters of religion and conscience, and the establishment and operation of disciplinary committees. The department is staffed by several officers and non-commissioned officers. The NCOs perform registry and administrative work under the professional supervision of the Deputy Chief Military Personnel Officer (DCMPO), but their supervisor is the commanding NCO of the mission.

Destruction of collected landmines in the Moroccan controlled area, 2009. (János Besenyő collection)

Planning and Operations Department

Although intelligence previously operated independently as a small office of 3–4 people under the leadership of the Chief Information Officer (CMIO), it was only capable of very limited activities.[17] Perhaps for this reason, at time of writing the reconnaissance (G2) and planning and operations department (G3) – mainly due to the lack of manpower – operate together. The work of the department is managed by the Chief Operation Officer (COPO). His tasks include all kinds of military planning within the mission, data collection, processing and evaluation of information, coordinating the daily work of military observers (patrol duty and other service tasks).

Logistics Department

As everywhere else, this department (lead by Senior Military Logistics Advisor/SMLA) probably has the biggest responsibility and burden, since fuel, food, drinking water, and other logistical materials are always needed. Due to the long distances, the materials are mostly transported by three Mi-8 helicopters and three Antonov-type transport aircraft, which requires daily contact and continuous coordination from the cooperating departments. Due to the extreme conditions, the usability of the equipment and tools used by peacekeepers is significantly shorter than in other operations, and this also presents serious challenges to those working in logistics.[18] The planes are rented by the UN together with the Ukrainian (prior to 2022) and Russian crews from their countries, usually for periods of six months.

The responsibility for logistical support primarily affects the civilian, in other words non-military part of the mission, which is understandable as military observers at the headquarters usually only spend four to six months in one position. Due to the special nature of the situation in the camps and sector command, only military observers carry out logistical work, while the civilian logistical service (Department of Field Support/DFS) is located at the headquarters. Civilian specialists (in collaboration with soldiers) provide the following services within the mission: vehicle repair and servicing, transportation, communications, financial and other administrative tasks.

Welfare and Coordination Department

This is the smallest section in the mission and is responsible for supplying the military observers with canteen goods (cigarettes, alcohol, sweets, etcetera), and organising and conducting leisure programmes in the entire area of the mission. Among their tasks are the accommodation of observers coming from the camps to Laayoune, the reception of new arrivals, the organisation and management of various military and protocol events (national holidays, giving awards, etcetera). They are in contact with Moroccan and Spanish hotels, travel agencies and other tourist organisations,

Supplies arrive at the Smara airport for the team sites in the northern sector. (János Besenyő collection)

A tanker delivering fuel to the mission's team sites. (János Besenyő collection)

Christmas volleyball match between the teams of the camps and the headquarters. (János Besenyő collection)

and through them they provide discount air tickets for officers going home on leave.

Communications Department

Since the mission serves in the territory of three countries, due to the area's incomplete infrastructure, the telecommunications specialists developed their own communication system independent of the mission's host states. Those serving in the communications department operate the radio (long and short wave, VHF and HF) and telephone systems in cooperation with civilian specialists (UN employees); they maintain and repair computer and news equipment (fax machines, computers, photocopiers, etcetera).

Health Department

Switzerland first offered a health unit to the MINURSO staff in 1991, with a staff of 85, which was soon reduced to 61.[19] The Swiss, working with three fixed-wing aircraft, provided full medical services (basic medical and dental care, as well as minor surgeries) to the peacekeepers in the entire area of the mission. The mission's medical centre was established at the headquarters, but well-equipped clinics were also set up in the cities of Dakhla and Smara. In January 1993, the Swiss reduced the size of the unit to 41 people, closed the clinic in the city of Dakhla, and transformed the Smara clinic into a medical centre, where only first aid and evacuation were carried out when necessary.[20] The experience of medical soldiers was often needed during the operation. For example, in Oum Dreyga camp, a Chinese peacekeeper was stung by a scorpion. Since there was no medical officer in the camp and the Chinese officer's condition was rapidly deteriorating, the Swiss military doctors were called from the mission command. The doctors arrived within two hours, then administered the antidote and the tetanus injection to the peacekeeper, who recovered within a few days.[21] In another case, on 18 January 1993, a patrol car of the peacekeepers collided with a Moroccan truck. In the accident, one peacekeeper lost his life immediately, and the other had to be evacuated with serious injuries. In the same year, a Swiss PC-6 Pilatus Porter aircraft crashed for unknown reasons on its way to the Dougaj team site. The Swiss pilot flying the plane, an Australian doctor, and a Norwegian technician who were travelling on it lost their lives immediately, the nurse who was with them was taken to the hospital in a critical condition.[22]

In 1994, the Swiss, together with the Canadians and Australians, discontent with the high cost and failure of the mission, announced that they would withdraw the medical unit by the end of June.[23] Since the member states did not offer a medical unit to replace the Swiss, they withdrew most of their troops on 18 June, but 10 voluntarily remained in the area until the UN resolved their replacement.[24] Finally, the Republic of Korea offered a 40-member strong medical team to Western Sahara, so the last group of Swiss medical soldiers could leave the mission in mid-August 1994.[25] The first Korean doctors arrived on 11 August, but the entire unit did not start operating until 3 October. Over the years, the unit's strength was reduced to 20, but the Korean Medical Unit (KMU) served in Western Sahara until 13 May 2006, when their tasks were taken

In the late 1970s, thanks to generous military subsidies from Saudi Arabia, the Royal Moroccan Army initiated a massive rearmament programme. Amongst others, it intended to acquire additional Panhard AML-90 armoured cars from France: the production line for these was in the process of being closed, and the Moroccans were referred to South Africa, where the AMLs were manufactured under licence as the Eland. Eventually, Rabat placed orders for South African-made AML-90s, and also for 80 of the then brand-new Ratel-20 infantry fighting vehicles and Ratel-90 armoured cars (the latter shown here). As of the early 2000s, more than 60 were still in operational service, all deployed in Western Sahara. (Artwork by David Bocquelet)

In the course of the same 'shopping spree', in 1978 Morocco acquired 111 SK-105 Kürassier light tanks from Austria. Based on a modified chassis of the Saurer armoured personnel carrier, these were equipped with an oscillating turret mounting the French 105mm 105G1 gun. Starting in 1979, Kürassiers were deployed with three armoured squadrons in Western Sahara: while a few were captured by Polisario, they remain in service until today. (Artwork by David Bocquelet)

One of the most numerous medium battle tanks of the Royal Moroccan Army deployed in the Western Sahara was the M48A3. The first of about 225 were delivered in 1973, and the last in 1987, by when most of the fleet was locally upgraded to the M48A5 standard, with help from US advisors. Weighing around 45,000kg when loaded for combat, the A5 variant included the M68 105mm gun in place of the original 90mm calibre M41), a metric-measurement M16 fire-control system, the more powerful AVDS-1750-2C RISE engine, and T142 tracks. (Artwork by David Bocquelet)

The principal armoured personnel carrier in service with the Royal Moroccan Army remains the US-made M113, which was acquired in huge numbers, including 400 M113A1/A2 and 419 M113A3. Most of them continue serving in their basic version, armed solely with a. 50-cal/12.7mm Browning M2 heavy machine gun (shown left). About 20 have been modified through the installation of the Soviet-made ZPU-2 twin-barrel 14.5mm heavy machine gun (shown right). (Artwork by David Bocquelet)

In addition to over 800 M113s, Morocco acquired at least 60 M163 Vulcan Air Defense System (VADS) self-propelled anti-aircraft guns, including the General Dynamics M61 Vulcan six-barrel 20mm cannon mounted on the M113 chassis. Although considered short-ranged in the West for its intended anti-aircraft role, the M163 proved highly popular in Morocco because of its high cyclic rate of fire, which can reach up to 3,000 rounds per minute, if deployed in short bursts of 10, 30, 60, or 100 rounds (continuous rate of fire is at 1,000 rounds per minute). Over 50 remain in service with the Royal Moroccan Army units deployed in Western Sahara: most of them have received locally manufactured sand skirts, as illustrated here. (Artwork by David Bocquelet)

The Canon de 155mm Mle F3 Automoteur was developed in the early 1950s in France. Mounted on the cassis of the AMX-13 light tank, it is the smallest and lightest self-propelled gun carriage ever manufactured. Its compact size and low cost resulted in considerable success on the export market. Morocco acquired 98 Mk F3s between 1978 and 1997, and around 90 of these remain in service with three artillery regiments usually deployed in Western Sahara. (Artwork by David Bocquelet)

The primary patrol vehicle of the MINURSO contingent in Western Sahara is the Toyota Land Cruiser Prado. This is a full-size, four-wheel drive vehicle in the Land Cruiser range, with a ladder frame chassis, two-speed transfer boxes and rear beam axles. The earlier J70-series of the 1990s was replaced by the J90 series in a five-door long-wheelbase version, as illustrated here. They are all painted in white overall, wearing large black UN insignia on their sides, and blue registration plates starting with prefix 'MIN'. (Artwork by David Bocquelet)

The Toyota Land Cruiser HJ47 light utility truck of the 1970s remains the primary combat vehicle of the Sahrawi People's Liberation Army (SPLA; often abbreviated as ELPS from the *Ejército de Liberación Saharaui*). Powered by a 3.6-litre or 4.0-litre inline six-cylinder diesel engine with an output of 95 horse powers, they have proven highly reliable, rugged vehicles, with an excellent range. Nearly all have their hardtop/driver cab removed, and most now mount ZU-23-2 twin 23mm anti-aircraft autocannons, as illustrated here. (Artwork by David Bocquelet)

Although seeing no action since 1991, the Soviet-made 9K31 (ZRK-BD Strela-1, NATO-reporting name 'SA-9 Gaskin') supplied by Libya remains one of the primary air defence weapons of the ELPS and is always shown in its military parades held in the Tindouf area, in south-western Algeria. Generally, they are painted in dark sand overall, usually enhanced through the addition of a disruptive pattern in olive green. The box-like missile containers for 9M31 or 9M31M missiles are usually left in olive green overall. (Artwork by David Bocquelet)

Generally, officers of the Hungarian Defence Forces assigned to MINURSO in Western Sahara were issued their usual 1990M four-colour ('woodland') camouflage uniform, introduced in 1994. The officer shown here wears the M90 Army Shirt with short sleeves (made of cotton), black textile belt, summer field pants, and M75 black or dark brown leather boots. As for all United Nations peacekeepers, the headgear consisted of a blue-coloured beret, usually made of 100 percent wool, and having a black leather band trim. (Artwork by Renato Dalmaso)

Based on the requirement to equip Hungarian Defence Forces contingents serving with UN peacekeepers in Cyprus and Western Sahara, a derivative of the 1990M woodland pattern was developed in the form of a desert camouflage uniform, usually referred to as 2004M. This uses the same shapes as the 1990M, but in sand, khaki, rosy brown, and russet brown instead of russet brown, olive green, light stone, and black (respectively). As standard for NATO armies, name tapes and rank patches (usually in tactical brown and tan) are worn atop of breast pockets, with a crest in national colours on the shoulder. (Artwork by Renato Dalmaso)

The Royal Moroccan Army uses several different types of uniforms. Shown here is the Red Lizard camouflage set of fatigues: based on the British paratroopers' Denison smock, this was first introduced by the French in 1947, and entered service in Morocco in the 1980s. The SPECTRA helmet of French design, but locally manufactured by MSA Mohammedia, has a cloth cover in the same camouflage pattern as the uniform, and this infantryman wears a cargo west with ammunition pouches and knee pads. Infantry smallarms include the US-made M4 carbine and M16 assault rifle. (Artwork by Renato Dalmaso)

Over time, the ELPS has sourced its equipment and gear from very different sources: in the 1970s and 1980s its primary supporter was Libya, which provided not only heavy arms, but also uniforms and personal gear. Amongst these was this two-piece camouflage uniform made of water-repellent cotton, the design of which was originally based on the OG-107 developed for the US Army in the 1950s. Colours included were blue-green, light green, and dark brown. (Artwork by Renato Dalmaso)

Having lost much international support from the 1970s and 1980s, the Sahrawi Arab Democratic Republic remains a partially recognised state, controlling only the easternmost fifth of the total territory of Western Sahara. Thus, the modern-day ELPS is still equipped with outdated weaponry of Soviet origin, and uniforms and other gear provided by Libya in the 1980s. This machine-gunner is shown as armed with the 9kg, Soviet-made 7.62mm PKM machine gun, and wearing a yellow scarf protecting him from sun and sand. (Artwork by Renato Dalmaso)

Shown during a meeting with MINURSO observers, this veteran ELPS officer is illustrated wearing a version of the OG-107 fatigues in olive drab: this uniform was originally designed in the USA in the 1950s, but has been manufactured in the polyester-cotton blend since the early 1970s. Originally supplied to the ELPS by Libya in the 1970s, it is now locally made. (Artwork by Renato Dalmaso)

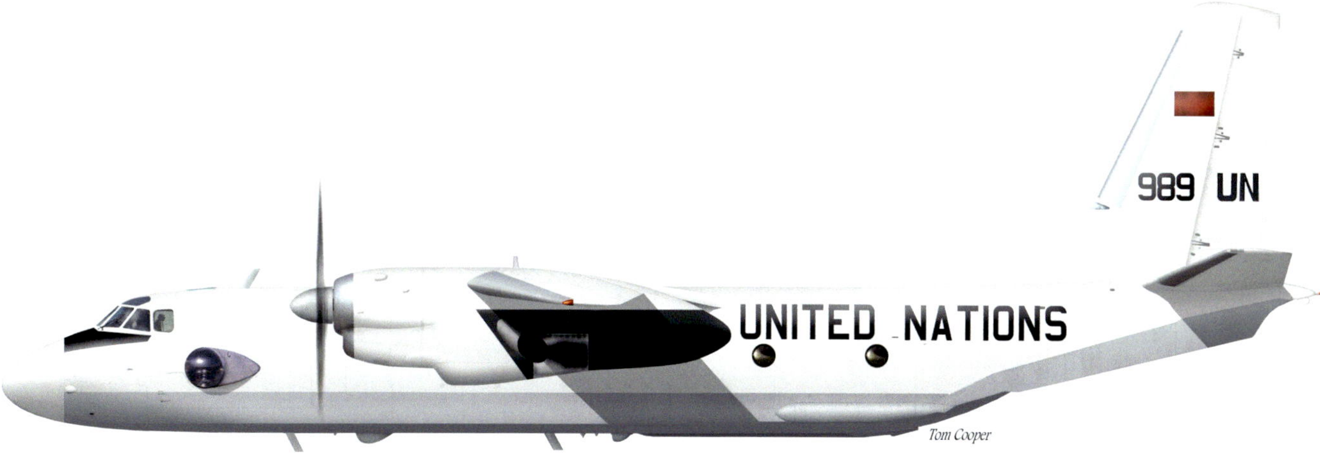

Because of the vast distances and isolation of its team sites, MINURSO is supported by several aircraft and helicopters. Amongst them were always two Antonov An-26s: the first two of these – including the example shown here, deployed in Western Sahara in the second half of the 1990s – were provided by Russia. They were replaced by two aircraft of the Romanian air force, and then by others. As usual, all were largely painted in white, and wore distinct (even if temporary) service titles. (Artwork by Tom Cooper)

As of the second half of the 1990s and through the first half of the 2000s, the MINURSO contingent included four Mil Mi-8 helicopters, mostly drawn from the Russian Air Force. All were painted in white overall, wore Russian flags and registration numbers – but the latter two were often applied in different fashion than shown here: flags on the fin, and registration numbers on intakes. All were equipped with weather radar in a bulb under the nose, and had a winch for search and rescue purposes. (Artwork by Tom Cooper)

While withdrawing from service its old and worn-out Northrop F-5A/B Freedom Fighters, the Royal Moroccan Air Force continued flying Northrop F-5E/F Tiger IIs. Through the 1990s and 2000s, they flew regular reconnaissance sorties over Western Sahara, usually equipped with Italian-made ELT-555 ECM pods (shown installed on the underwing pylon) as a self-protection measure against SA-6 and SA-8 surface-to-air missiles operated by the ELPS. Moroccan F-5E/Fs remained in service as of 2020–2022 and were in the process of being upgraded through the installation of Israeli-made sensors and weaponry. (Artwork by Tom Cooper)

A new Mi-8 helicopter being delivered to the mission area, being unloaded from an Antonov Volga-Dnepr An-124 cargo aircraft at Laayoune airport. (János Besenyő collection)

MINURSO peacekeepers on patrol. (János Besenyő collection)

Smara team site in 2003. (János Besenyő collection)

Collection of landmines for destruction in the Moroccan controlled area, 2009. (János Besenyő collection)

A UN vehicle involved in an accident while on patrol. (János Besenyő collection)

POLISARIO soldiers from the 4th Military Region with a vehicle mounted ZSU-23. (János Besenyő collection)

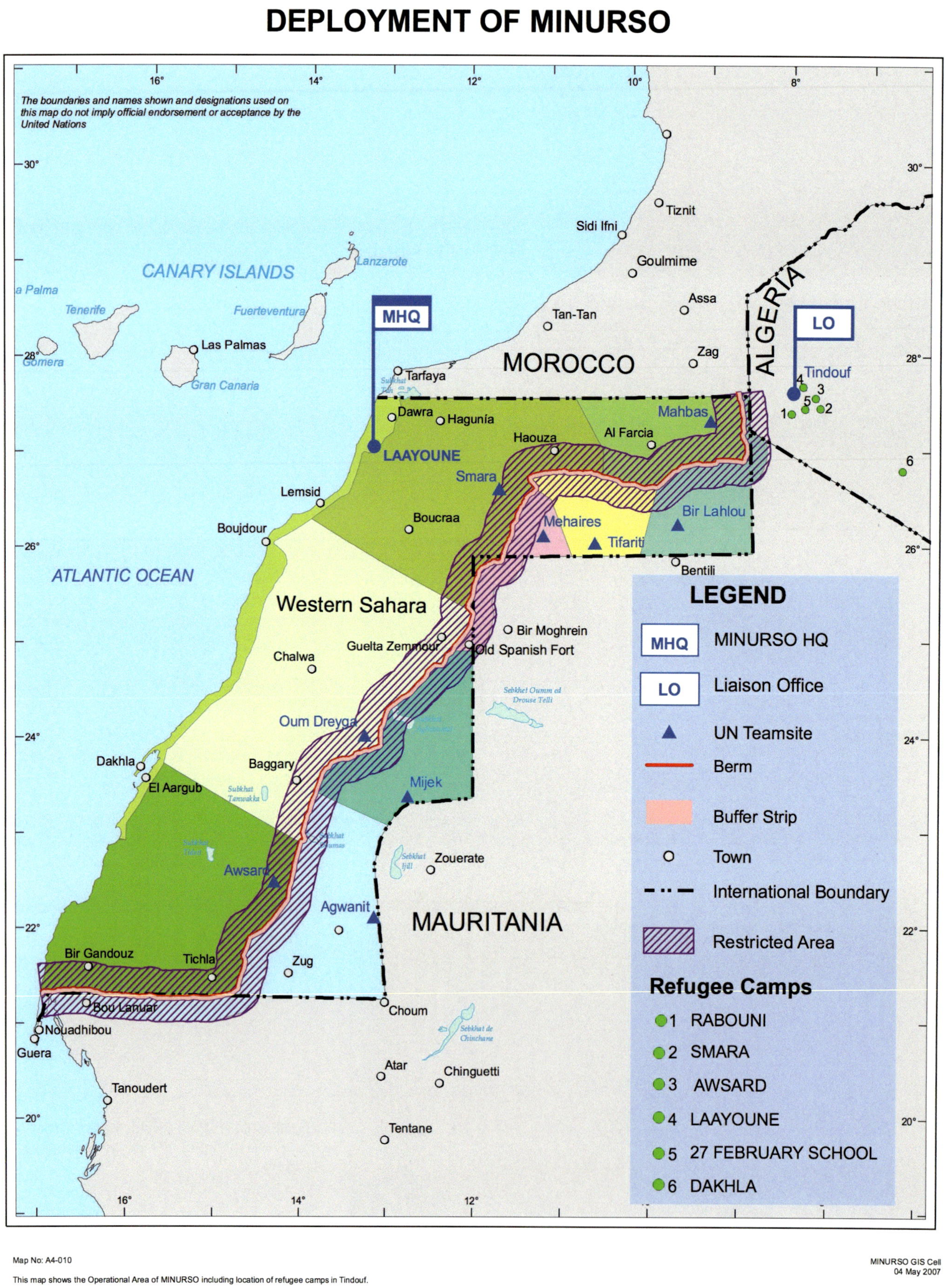

This map shows the operational area of MINURSO including locations of refugee camps in Tindouf. (United Nations with additional information from the author)

over by a Malaysian Medical Unit (MMU).[26] The Malaysian doctors served in the mission until the end of 2010,[27] they were replaced by a group of doctors from Bangladesh (Bangladesh Medical Unit/BMU).[28] Although the primary task of the medical teams is to provide healthcare to those serving in the mission, in some cases, they have also provided medical care to civilian residents who turn to them.[29]

Structure of the Organisation of the Camps

Usually, 12–20 people serve in the camps, but it also happens that only a fraction of them, six to seven people, serve in a given place, which makes work substantially difficult.[30] During the author's service, it often happened that due to the lack of personnel, the two patrols required per day were combined, and instead of eight, only four personnel performed the required task. Of course, this significantly increased the time spent on patrol. An average patrol consists of two all-terrain vehicles and four peacekeepers. In the camps, on average, two to three patrols must be carried out per day, which is increased by three to four aerial reconnaissance patrols per month.[31] The duration of patrol duty can range from a few hours to a few days, depending on the nature of the task and the distance. The basic purpose of the patrols is to monitor the observance of the ceasefire agreement and the military units of the opposing parties, to investigate and then report possible violations.[32] All of this is done in such a way that the opposing parties have repeatedly limited/restricted their free movement and hindered their activities.[33] The military observers here are on permanent duty, their only opportunity to rest is on maintenance day. At that time, the observers do not patrol, but perform repair and maintenance work in the camp area, after which they have more opportunities to rest than on an average day.[34] There are currently no camps in the area of the mission, as the Zoug camp was closed at the end of 1991,[35] and then the Dougaj camp by the mission command in August 1996,[36] and due to the termination of the sector commands, Dakhla was closed in 2005 and the military observers serving there were transferred to other camps.[37] Of course, it also happened that the camps had to be moved for security or other reasons, for example Mehairest, where there was no airfield of a suitable size near the old camp site where the Antonov-type aircraft could land.

The camps in the mission area, the work going on there, and the opposing forces are presented below.[38]

Smara

The patrol area of the camp is approximately 43,000km^2. The area between Laayoune and Smara has relatively easy-to-travel, well-developed roads, while from Smara to the wall system that represents the border, the area is divided by dry riverbeds, covered with volcanic stones, with unpaved roads. In the area of the camp and the sector, there is a section of more than 550 kilometres of the wall system, here is the military sector of the Moroccans (Saguia El Hamra-Laayoune), which is divided into further subsectors (Amgala, Smara, and Haouza). These subsectors were created to keep an eye on the Polisario Front's two strongest military districts, Military District 2 (Tifariti) and 5 (Bir Lahlou). The approximate size of military units stationed here is 30–35,000 people.

In the Smara area, the Moroccan army has nearly a hundred small and large strong points. An independent platoon or company serves in each strong point, under the authority of the Independent (static) Infantry Battalions (BIS) guarding the wall system. The strength of the formations stationed here is approximate 50–60 percent, their housing conditions are rudimentary, their food is not very good, but their combat morale is adequate. Soldiers serving here receive a 15-day leave to visit their families in Morocco after every four months of service. In reality, those serving in BIS formations are meant to hold off the attacking troops until a counterattack can be commenced. About 3–5 kilometres behind the strong points, the intervention units are stationed, whose task it is to push back the Polisario units carrying out an attack. These are mostly light and heavy armoured formations (120 M48s, and some units equipped with T-72 tanks permanently leased from Belarus), mechanised infantry and artillery units.[39] Although their morale is better and their strength reaches 75–80 percent, it has nevertheless been proven in practice that they are often slow against the guerrillas and why several times in the 1980s Polisario soldiers raided strong points, and by the time the intervention forces arrived, they had already retreated with their prisoners. The arriving Moroccan soldiers could only collect their dead. Of course, such actions only took place prior to the ceasefire, and although they had a great moral value for the Sahrawi guerrillas, they brought little in terms of military results. This can also be observed in the limited conflict that erupted at the end of 2020. Although the Saharawi guerrillas carried out several attacks against the Moroccan positions, they were unable to penetrate the wall system, and the damage they caused was not significant.[40]

A Moroccan strongpoint. (János Besenyő collection)

Part of the Berm, with one of the Moroccan strongpoints. (János Besenyő collection)

Moroccan M48A3 tanks on standby in one of the strongpoints. (János Besenyő collection)

In order to more effectively repulse potential intruders into the defensive wall system, the Moroccan leadership has stationed several units that can be immediately deployed as a reserve 10–25 kilometres away from the wall system. There are also the organisations that provide the logistical supply of the strong points and the headquarters here.

The military observers serving here have a relatively good relationship with the opposing parties, despite the fact that their work is often hindered by the representatives of the Moroccan army,[41] and on occasion they have pointed weapons at the military observers and even threatened to open fire on them.[42] Due to these and other similar events, on 18 September 1996, the Portuguese Major General José Eduardo Garcia Leandro, who was in charge of the military part of the mission, travelled to Agadir, where Southern Command of the Royal Moroccan Army was located. There he met with the leaders of the Moroccan army, who promised to hold accountable their officers and field officers who did not cooperate with the mission.[43] However, the peacekeepers did not experience much of this cooperation, as some of the Moroccan officers continued to obstruct their work. For example, the commander of the 64th Infantry Battalion outright forbade his officers to answer any questions of the military observers, while the commander of the Smara subsector, Major General Mouassaoui, did not assign a liaison officer to any of his units, so permission or any information had to be officially requested from him. Of course, in the majority of cases, the answer was a polite refusal, because the UN sector commander (Smara operated as a sector command for a while, but this system was abolished by the UN in 2005, citing economic reasons),[44] who was previously in the rank of colonel, and later the camp commander, were not of the same rank as him, and the general considered only the military commander of MINURSO to be of equal rank. The commander of the Amgala subsector, Major General Jerar and Colonel Mouzouri, the commander of the 28th Infantry Battalion, for example, refused to give an answer to the UN representatives because they believed that the military situation had not essentially changed since the beginning of the mission, and it was not their job to inform the UN representatives.

On the Polisario Front part, the movement of patrols is also often restricted, and access to certain areas is outright prohibited. The opposing parties often violate the existing ceasefire agreement, and the UN does nothing but send an official protest. For example, Northrop F-5E Tiger II fighter-bombers of the Royal Moroccan Air Force regularly make reconnaissance flights into the restricted zone, while Polisario soldiers dressed as civilians try to detect weak points in the wall system and minefields planted by the Moroccans. Due to the nature of the mission, the camp is not protected by an armed guard, however, there are also Moroccan military units in the area, so their soldiers guard the road leading to the UN facility and the entrance.

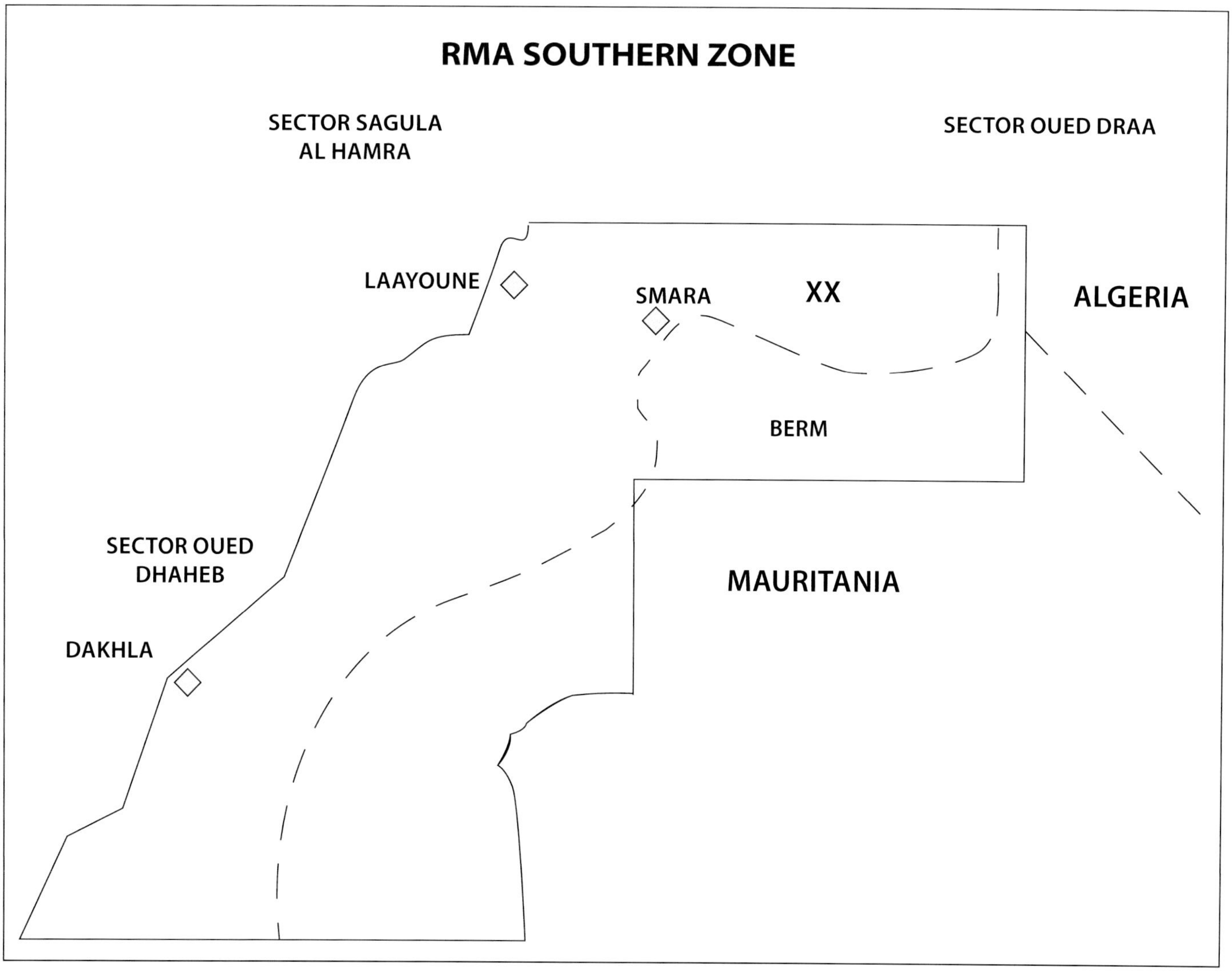

Southern Command of the Royal Moroccan Army. (Diagram by author)

The Smara camp has the longest patrol routes, and since the airport handles the logistics of the other camps in the northern region, the workload of the military observers on duty is very high.[45] The fact that part of the route of the Paris-Dakar Rally is located in the patrol area makes life especially difficult for those who serve here, and during the race, the Polisario Front often threatens the organisers with taking the participants of the race hostage. This may happen because the route also touches the territory they control, and they do not recognise the right of the Moroccans to control the territories they occupy, and they consider it an integral part of the Sahrawi Arab Republic (SADR). As the route of the competition touches the patrol areas of several camps (Smara and Mehaires) as well, during the competitions, military observers coordinated by the mission commander will monitor the course of the race throughout, and MINURSO Mi-8 helicopters are on standby with the designated medical team.

The race route runs from the Moroccan city of Tan-Tan to Smara, then through the subsectors of Smara and Amgala, in the direction of Bir Moghrein, cutting through the wall system. In the days leading up to the competition, military observers erect camps on both sides of the wall (usually from the Smara and Mehaires camps) from where they monitor the events for several days. With their presence, they try to prevent any incidents between Moroccan and Polisario soldiers during the competition. At the same time, most of the military observers from all the camps in the sector are sent to the competition area, where they continuously conduct aerial and ground reconnaissance (patrol service). Their experiences are reported immediately on the radio channel shared by MINURSO and the race organisers, so the competitors are always aware of the latest current events. Of course, despite the preparations, almost every year some unexpected event has occurred.

In January 2001, the Polisario Front leadership threatened the organisers of the race that competitors who crossed the territory without permission would be taken prisoner as the race organisers had not asked for their consent to pass through the area they controlled. The organising committee considered the threat to be frivolous and did not deal with the matter. The Polisario Front might have accepted the situation if the race had simply passed through territory under their control, but during preparation, a unit of Moroccan soldiers penetrated five kilometres into the Liberated Zone to pick up mines and unexploded ordnance along the route of the rally. During the demining, the Moroccan soldiers fired several shots in the direction of the nearby Polisario guard post, which violated the ceasefire agreement in force. At that time, the Polisario Front openly demanded that the UN immediately stop the competition and for the Moroccans to apologise. However, the leadership of MINURSO was not able to fulfil any of their demands, and they threatened the peacekeepers with military action.[46] In the days leading up to the race UN patrols reported that the Polisario Front had ordered full mobilisation in the 2nd, 4th, and 5th Military Districts. The soldiers of the organisation waited for orders, in uniform and fully armed, next to their vehicles, and they refused to talk to the military observers. The report of the observers was also confirmed by the unit sent by the Mauritanians, so the organisers took the threat seriously and asked for the help of the surrounding states to ensure the safety of the race. The Mauritanian government deployed an entire battalion from Bir Moghrein under the command of Major Mohamed Abdulah to secure the route of the race and push back any Polisario units that might invade their territory. Mehaires patrols met the Mauritanian soldiers, whose commander said they had been given orders to fire immediately in case the Polisario soldiers threatened the security of the race in any way. The major established another detachment, barely 20 kilometres from the border near the village of Echraga, which consisted of two companies of soldiers well-equipped with anti-aircraft weapons. In order to ensure the safety of the competitors, the Moroccans, in violation of the ceasefire agreement, carried out reconnaissance in the area of the competition with military aircraft.

Unfortunately, the Moroccan Chief of Staff held a press conference in haste where he questioned the Polisario Front's right to prevent the race. The General's reckless statement exacerbated the situation between the opposing parties. In response, the commander of the 4th Military District ordered an alert and deployed five vehicles equipped with ZPU-type anti-aircraft weapons with the aim of driving the invading aircraft back to Moroccan territory. At the same time, the Polisario Front leadership and all military district commanders demanded an immediate explanation from the UN and mission leaders regarding the General's statement. Since they did not receive a satisfactory answer, several provisions were introduced restricting the free movement and work of military observers (these measures were later only withdrawn at the request of the new military commander, Major General György Száraz, due to the good cooperation established with him).[47] Sahrawis living in European countries boarded planes en masse upon hearing the news of the Polisario Front mobilising, and after arriving in Tindouf, reported for service at the Polisario military command. At that time, the Moroccan army also began to mobilise, not only the troops stationed along the Berm were put on alert,[48] but also those stationed around Agadir.

It seemed that the outbreak of a new war was only a matter of hours away. At that time, the diplomats of the USA, France, and the AU, as well as the UN Secretary-General, Kofi Annan, put pressure on Algeria to stop the Sahrawis immediately. The Algerian Chief of Staff, General Mohamed Lamari, started direct negotiations with the Secretary-General of the Polisario Front, Mohammed Abdelaziz, who managed to get out of the uncomfortable situation by saying that if the organisers of the competition officially request permission from the Saharawis, armed conflict could be avoided. Then, Eagleton, the organiser of the race, sent his representative, Mr Roger Kalmanovitz, to Tindouf, where he finally agreed with the leaders of the SADR to continue the competition.[49] The Sahrawi militants then retreated to their precincts and the race ended without incident. Perhaps ever since then, the opposing parties have never come so close to the re-emergence of the conflict. In the same race, one of the Portuguese competitors ran onto an anti-tank mine near the Berm. He was rescued by a UN plane and a medical team and transferred to the Naval Hospital in Las Palmas. The competitor's car had deviated from the path regularly used by military observers by about 15 metres: the driver's leg later had to be amputated.[50]

The organisation of the race to be held in 2003 began during the 11th congress of the Polisario Front ('Natasha' action). Between 13–15 October the department preparing the race, Moroccan and Mauritanian soldiers, as well as military observers representing

Major General György Száraz, Force Commander of MINURSO between 2002 and 2005. (János Besenyő collection)

A camp of peacekeepers deployed to ensure the Paris-Dakar race next to one of the supply points near Mehaires in 2004. (János Besenyő collection)

Competitors of the Lisboa-Dakar rally with the peacekeepers in 2007. (János Besenyő collection)

the UN, went through the planned route of the car race. The organisers, even though they had contacted the Polisario Front that year, were afraid of its actions, but did not want to jeopardise the diplomatic successes achieved and so the preparatory work went unhindered. They wished the competitors good luck, and the rally concluded peacefully. The only problem during the race was that the Mauritanian soldiers demanded US$50 in cash from each vehicle that crossed the border. Although the organisers protested against the 'robbery', the border guards made everyone pay the newly introduced 'border crossing fee.' In recent years, the races held here have become ever riskier, mainly due to the strengthening of the Salafist movement linked to Al-Qaeda, who have repeatedly carried out armed attacks not only against foreign tourists, but also against Mauritanian soldiers.[51]

Mahbas

The camp at Mahbas is located in Moroccan territory, and there is also an airport nearby from which Tindouf is served. Those who serve here control an area of approximately 12,500km^2, and their area of responsibility covers more than 250km of the Moroccan defensive wall system. The area of the camp borders the Moroccan state border to the north, the strong point system/Berm to the south, the Algerian state border and parts of the Berm to the east, and the Houza subsector to the west. The patrol area is mostly stony, in some places there are insignificant elevations and smaller continuous, hard-to-walk, sandy sections. On the other hand, there are several continuous mountain ranges in the vicinity of the Berm, where it is difficult to get around even with an off-road vehicle. The settlement of Mahbas is located close to the camp, where approximately 300 people live. The village is connected by a paved road to the area's largest reservoir at Zag, where the Spanish had also operated a military station. There are 44 existing wells in the area, however, the water of most of these is only suitable for animals, or too salty to drink at all.

There two Moroccan subsectors of Mahbas and Farsia are in the area of the camp, the number of troops stationed there is approximately 13,000. In these subsectors, the units are usually at 60–70 percent strength as some of the soldiers serving here are constantly on leave. The two subsectors contain the following weapons:

- armoured cars and infantry fighting vehicles (French AML-60 and AML-90, South African Ratel-20 and Ratel-90 types)
- armoured fighting vehicles (American M48 and Belarusian T-72 tanks)
- self-propelled artillery and multiple rocket launchers (M101, M109, F3, and BM-21)
- trucks, jeeps

The personal weapons of the soldiers stationed at Mahbas are very well maintained, mostly from American and French sources. The living conditions of the soldiers are often worse than in other subsectors, which is also reflected in the fact that the daily water ration, for both drinking and washing, of those serving here is barely five litres. Despite the difficult conditions, the morale of the personnel is surprisingly good. The weapons of the formations are from a variety of sources including German, French, American, and Russian, and a significant part of them are of old manufacture but well-maintained. Units regularly participate in various training exercises, usually with platoon, company, and battalion strength. Although the exercises are announced under existing agreements, military observers or other personnel of the UN are strictly denied participation or supervision of the exercise. The exercises usually involve locating enemy units that have infiltrated the area through guerrilla methods, followed by their complete elimination.

Due to heavy fighting in this area, there are several areas that are heavily contaminated with unexploded artillery shells and mixed anti-personnel and anti-armour mines. Although the ordnance and mines found in the area are destroyed by the Moroccan army within a relatively short period of time, due to their frequent occurrence, they have repeatedly caused accidents amongst the soldiers and the Bedouins. For example, in June 1994, a MINURSO patrol car ran onto a mine that exploded, though fortunately, the Uruguayan peacekeeping officer in the car was not seriously injured.[52] Less than a month after that incident there was another involving peacekeepers where on 5 July 1994, a vehicle patrolling northeast of Mahbas ran onto an anti-tank mine and then exploded, as a result of which one of the peacekeepers had to be evacuated with life-threatening injuries, the other observer fortunately only suffered minor injuries.[53]

Another incident took place in the camp at Mahbas, involving a Hungarian peacekeeper who had an accident while on patrol with a fellow officer from an African country. The African officer suffered serious injuries, so the Hungarian soldier gave him first aid. Unfortunately, the first aid box contained only very basic equipment and many things were missing, including rubber gloves. The mission's military doctors praised the Hungarian officer, who for a few days was thought of as a 'brave first-aider', after which, however, it turned

Major Tamás Hárs with the helicopter crew in volved in the communications misunderstanding. (János Besenyő collection)

Mahbas team site in 2010. (János Besenyő collection)

out that the injured man he was caring for was infected with the HIV virus. After that, attitudes changed and the epithet 'stupid' was used instead of 'brave' in relation to his actions. It took almost two months before test results proved he had not contracted the infection when giving first aid but during the waiting period he lost more than 10 kilogrammes in weight.

Several Hungarian soldiers served in this camp and almost all of them have an interesting story. Major Tamás Hárs served in Western Sahara in 2005/2006 as deputy commander of the Smara camp. During the missions, the soldiers often found themselves in a situation where they misunderstand or mishear the expressions of the foreign language they use as a service language. People often easily misunderstand words even in their native language, especially as a result of various hindering circumstances. There was one such case when the duty officer in the Smara camp (with barely three months of mission service), the pilot of the Mi-8 helicopter stationed at the Smara airport, and the duty officer in the Mahbas camp near Smara tried to communicate with each other by radio. The persons mentioned were all of different nationalities, and it should be understood, although it is not an excuse, that the conversations were conducted on radios and telephones, which, taking into account a foreign language (English), offers a serious possibility of misunderstanding the spoken words.

The procedure for receiving and launching a helicopter requires a Peacekeeper at the airport – in this case an air traffic control officer – who is responsible for the condition of the runway and who reports the arrival and departure of a helicopter to the duty officer. The duty officer reports this information to air traffic control at mission command. The helicopter pilot requests permission to take off from the flight controllers through the officer on. Sometimes, if warranted by weather conditions, the helicopter crew may request information from the duty officer of their position about the conditions (physical, weather, etcetera) at the landing site of the destination.

One example of such an exchange is detailed below:

Helicopter (H): 'Smara Duty Room, Smara Duty Room, this is Mi-8, I need permission!' [The helicopter pilot asks the duty officer to ask the air traffic controllers for permission to take off] (this conversation was over the radio)

Smara Duty Room (S): 'Mahbas Duty Officer, this is Smara Duty Officer, I need *condition*!' [Misunderstanding the pilot, the Smara duty officer asked the duty officer of the helicopter's next destination for information about the status of the landing site there] (via telephone)

Mahbas Duty Room (M): 'Smara Duty Officer, this is Mahbas Duty Officer, *condition* is good!' [Mahbas duty officer informs Smara duty officer that the landing site is in good condition] (via phone)

(S): 'Mi-8, this is Smara Duty Room, *condition* is good!' (via radio)

(H): 'Is *permission* good, granted?' (via radio)

(S): 'Yes, *condition* is good!' (via radio)

And the helicopter, in the operational area, took off without permission ... After that, the air traffic controllers naturally asked Major Hárs to explain what had happened. It took a lot of effort to track down the misunderstanding. The only thing that was more difficult was to 'cover up' the case.[54] Of course, there was experience gained: in this case, this misunderstanding did not represent a big risk, but in other circumstances it may have been different. Perhaps this case could have been avoided with stricter compliance with the rules of traffic control and greater care.

Mehaires[55]

The camp at Mehaires is located in an area controlled by the Polisario Front, which controls the territory of the 4th Military District and the troops stationed there. An important transport and trade route also runs here, due to which relatively lively civil activity involving Bedouins and traders can be observed. The military observers serving here patrol an area of 12,000km^2 on a daily basis with patrols lasting up to 10–12 hours.[56] The patrol area is bounded from the north-east by the Berm. One of the most important crossing points between the Moroccan and Polisario areas is located just 63 kilometres from the camp. The presence of the gate and the good condition of the roads leading here ensure relatively fast transport between the camp and the town of Smara. The natural characteristics of the area are extremely varied, from stony and rocky landscapes to sandy deserts, almost every landscape characteristic of the Sahara can be found. There are three settlements in the area.

Bir Moghrein is a border town in Mauritania with about 2,800 inhabitants and a garrison of 300 soldiers. The city also houses the office of the governor of the administrative area. The area's only paved airport operates here, but it is in such bad condition that it can only accommodate helicopters. Every Monday between 14:00 a.m. and 16:00 p.m., a radio link is established between the governor and the UN camp.

Hasi Locar is a very small settlement with about 250–300 inhabitants in the territory of Mauritania. Because of the nearby wells, the number of Bedouins settling in the city for a longer or

Polisario soldiers from the 4th Military Region. (János Besenyő collection)

MINURSO patrols meet with the Sahrawi soldiers, from whom they receive information – about the security situation in the given area, the activities of migrants or various smugglers and armed groups – over a cup of tea. (János Besenyő collection)

Saharawi nomads inside the Liberated Zone of Western Sahara. (János Besenyő collection)

shorter period of time is significant (approximately 100–150 people). There is an airport here as well, which can accommodate aircraft larger than helicopters (i.e. Antonovs), despite the fact that it does not have a solid surface.

El Hafira has a relatively small population (150 people), but it is the commercial centre of the area, where a big portion of the Bedouins and Polisario soldiers can buy the goods they need. There is a well-organised smuggling network in the city (cigarettes, food, etcetera). There are also several Bedouin families living around the city.

There are six airports in the Mehaires area that are suitable for receiving UN planes: Bir Moghrein, Mehaires, Motlani, Hasi Locar, Steila and Guelb Char. Airports are checked by patrols several times a month and any errors are reported to headquarters. Currently, all airports are capable of receiving UN aircraft, although the one at Bir Moghrein is only to a limited extent. There are several minefields scattered in the area and almost everywhere in the 5km buffer strip in front of the Berm, so mines and unexploded artillery shells pose a real danger to the patrols.

According to the official position, more than 1,000 soldiers serve in the district, but according to the experience of military observers, only a part of them are actually located in the districts and observation points. Polisario soldiers serving here are known to use the following types of weapons: ZPU, 82mm recoilless guns, 12.7mm machine guns, ZPU-1 and ZPU-2 14.5mm machine guns, and AK-47 assault rifles. It follows from the above that the soldiers of the 4th Military Region possess light weaponry, which are suitable for guerrilla warfare, but not for serious defensive or offensive battles.

In Mehaires, it was the custom to inaugurate a 'tombstone' in honour of someone who was transferred to another camp, indicating that he had successfully completed his task in Mehaires. In the picture is the 'tombstone ceremony' for the 'Hungarian Terminator' Major Béla Tamási, who served first as the commander of Mehaires team site and later deputy head of Tindouf in 2003. (János Besenyő collection)

Tifariti

The camp at Tifariti is located next to the small town of the same name, along an important route. The military observers serving here monitor the 2nd Military District and the troops subordinate to it. The area is rocky in the north, interspersed with small and large mountains, while classic desert conditions dominate in the south.

The patrol area of the camp is 12,000km^2, the camp is 75km from the Berm, and the northern border of Mauritania is 15km away. The command of the 2nd Military District is located in the village of Tifariti, and the subordinate units located in the area are detailed below. The equipment and weapons of the units are relatively weak and show a very mixed picture, and they do not operate at full strength as the majority of the soldiers stay in the Algerian refugee camps with their families. This district has perhaps the most capable and best trained units. According to intelligence, there is also a radar station operating in the area which is not officially included in its military order.

The combined military exercises of the Polisario units and the so-called 'people's' conferences are usually held in this area. One such large military exercise was held on 25 January 2003, involving the 2nd Military District (Tifariti), the 4th Military District (Mehaires) and the 5th Military District (Bir Lahlou). During the exercise, which lasted several days, the soldiers practiced the special 'hit and run' tactic, with the participation of an armoured battalion. The observers saw several armoured personnel carriers and other mostly Soviet/Russian-made tanks (T-55 and T-72), 60 jeeps equipped with ZPU-2 autocannons, some mortars and medium-sized guns (both field and anti-aircraft guns). The military commander of MINURSO, the northern sector commander, and several military observers also participated in a part of the exercise. They had the opportunity to meet the President of the Sahrawi Arab Republic, the Minister of Defence, and the commanders of the military districts. The military commander responsible for conducting the exercise was the commander of the 2nd Military District, Ibrahim Mohamed Biydillah. His personality as a military leader is interesting not only because he served as a logistics commander in the war, or because he was the Minister of Defence of the SADR until February 1999, but because his brother was appointed by the Moroccan ruler Mohamed VI as Minister of Health in November 2002.

Technical training (mine clearance, special explosion skills, etcetera) plays an increasingly important role in the training of the soldiers, and they do not hide the fact that they consider the occupation of the Moroccan combat positions on the Berm line and the infiltration of the occupied territories to be part of their tactics. Interestingly, urban guerrilla warfare or possible sabotage actions against Moroccan offices are considered unthinkable, as they rightly fear that such actions would be declared as terrorist activities, and the Moroccan troops – with the support of the Americans and the international community – would immediately launch a full offensive against them. In this case, the Polisario Front would lose its existing rights and opportunities as a legal diplomatic and liberation movement recognised by several countries to win independence or a possible autonomy. Although at the end of 2020, there was another limited armed conflict between the opposing parties, no such action was launched by the Polisario Front, despite the fact that it has sympathisers in the occupied territories.

According to information from the UN, there were Moroccan prisoners of war in several places in the district, who were forced to do various maintenance and fortification work. Cooperation between the military observers stationed here, the residents of the town, and the Polisario soldiers is very good, several joint programmes have been organised (dinners, visiting the local museum, etcetera), and the observers also provide financial support to several families with small children.

Bir Lahlou

This is one of the least loved stations in the northern sector, as the water here is extremely salty, so it is only suitable for ablution, but people are still advised to rinse themselves with mineral water afterwards. The climate of the area is extraordinarily extreme, the hottest temperatures were measured here (62°C). Due to the size of the district (36,000km^2), the patrol routes are relatively long, in the north the terrain is rather rocky, while in the south it is desert, interspersed with a few small mountains. There are several large dry lakes in the area. It is bordered to the north by the Moroccan wall system (Farsia and Mahbas subsectors), to the east by Algeria and Mauritania, to the south by Mauritania, and to the west by the 2nd Military District (Tifariti).

Those serving in Bir Lahlou control the 5th Military District and its associated units. The official number of people in the region is 1,100, but only a part of them resides in the districts. The Polisario soldiers mainly use ZSU-23-4, ZPU-1, ZPU-2, SA-9 Gaskin type weapons in this district. Most of the personnel use AK-47 assault

Moroccan prisoners of war, imprisoned for several years, being released in 2003. (János Besenyő collection)

Soldiers of the 2nd Military District (Tifariti) of the SADR taking part in a military exercise in 2002. (János Besenyő collection)

rifles, but French and American-made handguns captured from those serving here can also be seen. Although no major military exercises have been organised in the area for years, training and maintenance of military buildings and defensive positions are carried out continuously. The soldiers' weapons are in good condition, and their clothes – although they come from several sources such as Algeria, Libya – are still clean and well-kept. Perhaps the most experienced commanders and units of the Polisario Front can be found in this district. Several of the district's military leaders have served almost since the beginning of the war, most of them in Algeria, but there are also those who obtained military education in Cuba, Spain, and even the late Soviet Union. Despite the fact that old soldiers with battlefield experience and reliability were placed in the leading positions, rejuvenation can be increasingly observed within the organisation.

There are several military leaders within the organisation who, during the Spanish era, began their service with the nomadic troops, the Spanish Legion, or the local police forces, and then transferred to the Polisario Front after the withdrawal of the Spanish.

There are 69 permanently used wells in the patrol area (50 percent of the wells have water suitable for human consumption) and two small villages that are regularly visited by the patrols. Due to its central location the village of Bir Lahlou is considered

Bir Lahlou team site in 2002. (János Besenyő collection)

an important settlement with approximately 120–150 inhabitants. It also handles a lot of through-traffic, as the road connecting the towns of Rabouni and Agwanit passes through here. The village has more than 25 shops, a gas station and a repair shop. The UN camp and the airport are also nearby. Bentili is home to only 80–120 permanent residents and some temporarily settled Bedouin families live in this place. Next to the settlement there is an abandoned French Foreign Legion fortress and an airport maintained by the UN for the eventual evacuation of camps in the northern sector. Although it is not solidly covered, it is still suitable for receiving both Antonovs and Mi-8 helicopters. In many cases, the commander of the district restricts the free movement of military observers, thus, for example, he banned reconnaissance flights in the Bentili and Tersel districts. The patrols were only allowed to move in the area without a liaison officer between 1993 and 1994, and since then they can only travel with an escort designated by the local commander of the Polisario Front. When the observers check the military units, they must stop about 200 metres away from the camps, and then they can talk to the arriving commander, but most of their questions remain unanswered.

Dakhla

Previously, Dakkhla functioned as the centre of the southern sector, though later only as a camp, similarly to Smara. MINURSO operates a two-person military liaison office here. The city remains important to the mission due to its strategic location and role.

Perhaps one of the most diverse areas in terms of landscape, everything from the ocean to the classic desert can be found in the area. Due to the southern location, the temperature is very high during summer: the highest daytime temperature measured by military observers was 62°C, while the air usually cools down to 25–30°C at night. During winter, the average daytime temperature is only around 30–40°C, while at night it is around 5–10°C. In addition to patrolling, the duty of those serving here was to control, manage, and supply the camps in the southern sector. In the Oued Dhaheb sector, the Royal Moroccan Army has five subsector commands as follows: Tichla, Bir Gandouz, Awsard, Al Baggary and Oum Dreyga. The subsector commands operate independently and are divided into further subcommands.

Former French Foreign Legion Fortress Bentili visited by MINURSO peacekeepers. (János Besenyő collection)

Independent Infantry Battalions (BIS) are stationed on the Berm line and guard the fortifications and observation points located there. The weapons used by the battalions include 82mm recoilless guns, 23mm ZU-23 anti-aircraft guns, various types of heavy and light machineguns, and AML-90 armoured cars and AMX-13 light tanks.

The Mechanised Intervention Regiment (RIM) is located about 5–10 kilometres behind the infantry battalions, which can be deployed immediately after an attack on the wall and the fortifications. Their task is to stop the invading units, dislodge them from the occupied positions, and then stabilise the situation. These formations are provided with Land Rovers equipped with ZU and ZPU-type autocannons. They also have armoured personnel carriers such as the M113 and the M577 command version, and trucks with light cannons and rocket launchers. Next to the regiments – but not subordinate to them – artillery and anti-aircraft artillery units are also established, usually at the company or battalion level (Royal Artillery Group, GAR). Their task is to provide effective fire support for RIM units and destroy the attackers' artillery. Their armament includes artillery and mortars of various sizes (82mm, 105mm, 122mm, 155mm), ZU and ZPU autocannons and heavy machine guns, self-propelled anti-aircraft artillery (20mm) and heavy machineguns.

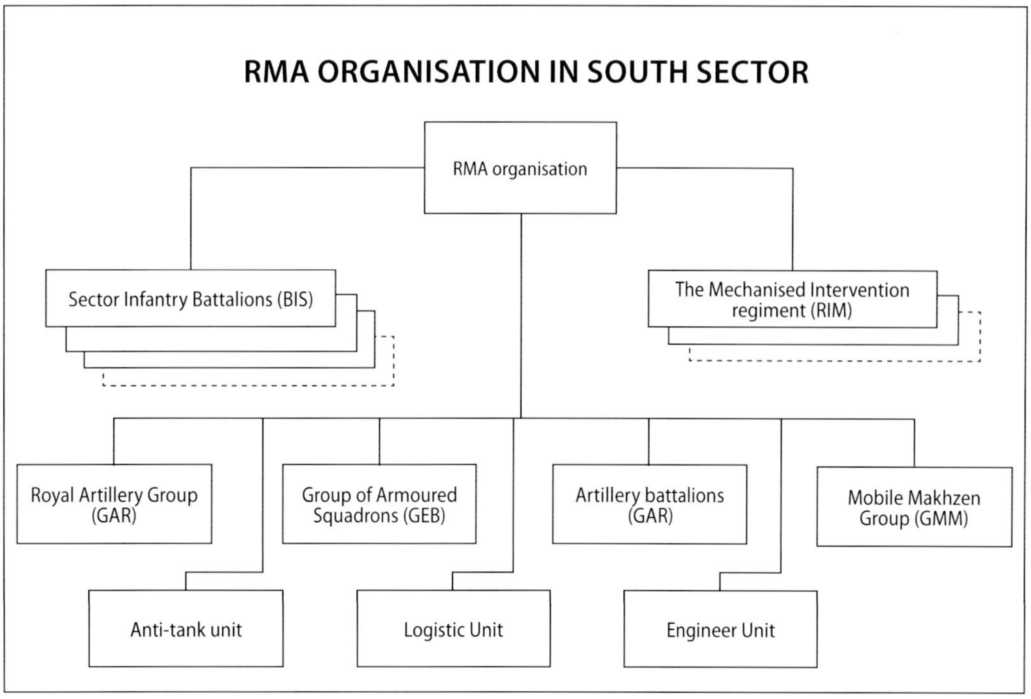

The structure of the Moroccan troops stationed in the area. (Diargram by the author)

Special units (Mobile Makhzen Group, GMM) are also established together with the regiments, which operate at a battalion level. Their task is to pursue and destroy the enemy that has been overrun. These units were created by General Ahmed Dlimi at the beginning of the 1980 Operation Uhud. The general's goal was for the units, which mostly consist of Sahrawis loyal to Morocco, to use the same combat tactics as the Polisario Front to successfully fight against the SADR militants who use guerrilla tactics. Almost 80 percent of the units are Sahrawi, who are paid slightly more by the government than average Moroccan soldiers.

There is also an airbase in the Dakhla area, where Moroccan Air Force Lockheed C-130 Hercules, Boeing CH-47 Chinooks, Aerospatiale SA.330 Pumas, and Bell UH-1 Hueys are stationed. In addition, of course, there are smaller and larger airstrips in the sectors that are capable of receiving aircraft. Due to the proximity of the ocean, Osprey 55-class and Cormoran-class gunboats of the navy regularly patrol the coastal waters in an attempt to prevent the Polisario Front's men from capturing fishing boats that do not have a permit from the SADR.[57] Along the coastline between the cities of Dakhla and Noadibou the 2nd Marine Battalion is on duty, and its units check coastal fishing villages and bays during their patrols. The battalion settles with independent companies near strategically important points.

There are two more refugee camps on the Moroccan side at Boujdour with 4,000 people, and Dakhla with 6,000 people, which are regularly visited by military observers. Refugees are provided 200 dirhams ($20) per month by the Moroccan government to keep them in the camps. However, this amount does not ensure a decent living, so a good number of refugees are literally destitute.

On the Polisario side are the 1st, 3rd, and 7th Military Districts, which are monitored by military observers stationed in the camps Agwanit and Mijek. In contrast to the Moroccan side, very few soldiers are on duty in these districts, rather they only monitor the Berm.

Awsard

The camp at Awsard is located in an area controlled by the Moroccan army. The district of responsibility of the camp is an area of 47,000km^2, where the surface is mostly rocky and covered with sand.[58] Patrol routes are usually long and often difficult to navigate. In the district, the Moroccan army has three subsectors: Bir Gandouz, Tichla, and Awsard. The number of Moroccan soldiers serving here is 12,000–13,000. The training and equipment of the units is adequate, and the morale of the soldiers is very good. The relationship between the leaders of the Moroccan units and the military observers is correct. There are 60 minefields in the district, mostly in the area in front of the fortification system. As the war saw several clashes between Moroccans and Polisario militants, unexploded artillery shells and planted mines were found in several places. For greater efficiency, the mines were mostly installed near wells and oases, as well as around heavily used roads. Moroccan technical units are constantly destroying the mines and artillery shells they find, but accidents still happen. For example, on 25 January 1992, one of the MINURSO patrol cars ran onto a mine, but fortunately the peacekeepers travelling in it suffered only minor injuries.[59] It was also here where one of the most serious accidents of the mission occurred, when the PC-6 aircraft of the Swiss medical personnel crashed for unclear reasons and all but one person on board lost their lives.[60] The patrols also regularly check the wells in the area, although only a few of them contain water suitable for human consumption. Near the camp is the small town called Awsard, where there are more than 100 residential buildings, a primary school, a telephone exchange, a hospital, and other administrative buildings. Despite this, only a few hundred civilians (mostly relatives of the soldiers serving here) live in the area, even with the Bedouin who are constantly on the move. Since this camp also provides logistical support to the other camps in the southern region, the workload of the military observers on duty is very high.[61]

Oum Dreyga

The camp at Oum Dreyga is in Moroccan territory, bounded by the Smara camp district to the north, the Berm to the east, and Awsard district to the south. Its patrol area is mainly made up of sandy soil,

Mines found around Awsard team site before destruction. (János Besenyő collection)

MINURSO peacekeepers gather for morning briefing at Awsard team site, 2004. (János Besenyő collection)

but smaller mountains can also sporadically be found here. The sand causes the most problems around the Berm, so much so that it makes patrolling impossible because the vehicles sink and are unable to go any further. Due to the military units located in the area and the proximity of the Berm, there are no civilian settlements or Bedouin camps in the area at all and only very rarely do the patrols encounter a few passing Bedouins. The area includes the three sectors under the Dakhla District: Guelta Zemmour, Oum Dreyga, and Al Baggary. The sectors are further divided into three or four subsectors, each of which is controlled by an infantry battalion, in other words, at least four mechanised infantry battalions must be considered per sector. In addition to infantry, there are also armoured and artillery units in the subsectors. The majority of the armoured personnel are located in built-up positions on the Berm line, while the artillery is installed a few kilometres further back.

Infantry units have jeeps equipped with heavy machine guns (like ZPU-1, ZPU-2, and ZPU-4), or with light machine guns; Willys jeeps equipped with 82mm recoilless rifles; and trucks equipped with ZPU heavy machine guns, or with ZU-23 autocanons. Armoured units use SK-105 light tanks and AML-90 armoured cars, and M113 armoured personnel carriers and their M577 command version. AU.50 (105mm) and Mk. F.3 (155mm) self-propelled artillery pieces, and BM-21 Grads (122mm) can be observed in the artillery units.

Military observers serving here monitor various military exercises, the maintenance of fortifications and other structures, and the destruction of any mines found. It is a relief for those serving on the Moroccan side that the Royal Army's bomb disposal units destroy the mines found by the observers relatively quickly, while demining in the areas controlled by the Polisario Front is only carried out to a limited extent due to lack of expertise and equipment. Because of this, not only the locals, but also the peacekeepers are at risk. In 2009, a patrol car launched from the camp ran onto a mine in the area controlled by the Moroccans and was damaged beyond repair. Fortunately, only one of the four peacekeepers travelling in the vehicle suffered minor injuries, but within a few weeks he was able to work again.[62]

Agwanit

The size of the patrol area of Agwanit is 37,000km^2, the area is bordered on the west by the Berm, on the east and south by the Mauritanian border, and on the north by the Mijek camp's area of responsibility. The terrain is very sandy, which makes patrolling difficult, but there are several areas covered with stones and some small mountains in the area. The climate is dry and extremely windy, and sandstorms are common in the summer months. The temperature is around 25–55°C in summer and 10–35°C in winter. There are 42 wells in the area, but only four of them have water suitable for consumption, and the water in the others is salty to the point of being undrinkable. Observers often meet the Bedouins living here, who call themselves 'es-sahel', whose four groups – the Cheilk, Daouad, Moussa, and Souaad – live in the countryside.

The wreckage of a crashed Avro Shackleton maritime patrol aircraft, as found near the Awsard team site. (János Besenyő collection)

Despite the utmost care, it is possible that a patrol vehicle will break down, in which case the peacekeepers try to eliminate the fault and then return the vehicle to the camp, where it is repaired by qualified vehicle mechanics. (János Besenyő collection)

This off-road vehicle of the peacekeepers serving in the Agwaniti camp stalled while on patrol. (János Besenyő collection)

Their estimated number is 320–350 people. In the 1st Military District, there are several infantry companies, a staff company, as well as logistics and fire support units. The estimated number of troops stationed here is 1,000, who use Land Rover and Toyota Land Cruiser type all-terrain vehicles, most of which are equipped with ZU-23-2 and ZPU-1 type autocannons. Military observers also saw an all-terrain vehicle equipped with AA heavy machinegun in the area. The fire support unit also has BM-21 type multiple rocket launchers and SA-9 'Gaskin' type air defence systems.[63] There are several observation points in the area that control the Moroccan fortifications. Observation points are usually manned by 5–8 soldiers equipped with light weapons and radios.

The 7th Military District has several mechanised infantry battalions, an artillery battalion, and a logistics company. Infantry battalions have five companies, while artillery battalions usually have two batteries. This district has better military equipment than the 1st Military District and its soldiers are also better trained. The old BMP-1 IFV type combat vehicles that make up the main armament are well maintained, and the infantry battalions also use several all-terrain vehicles equipped with ZU-23-2, ZPU-1, and ZPU-2 guns. Military observers have seen several D-30 122mm towed guns, BM-21 rocket launchers, and SA-9 'Gaskin' anti-aircraft systems with the artillery battalion.

The Polisario Front has several observation points in the area. There is no significant activity in the two districts except for the annual joint military exercise and the two live fire exercises. The cooperation between the military observers and the militants serving here can be considered good, however, the restrictive measures introduced by the locals make the work of the military observers difficult. If the military observers go on patrol duty, they must inform the commander of the 1st District by letter about the planned route 48 hours beforehand, while the information sent by the liaison officer is sufficient for the commander of the 7th District. Even though the commander of the 7th District is more helpful and cooperative with the UN observers, more restrictions have been put in place in both districts. It is forbidden to approach observation points, camps, ask questions of Sahrawi soldiers, or even use binoculars. Observers know the locations of six contiguous minefields, but mines or unexploded artillery shells have been found in another 51 locations, which remain a serious threat to local residents and UN workers.

Mijek

Military observers monitor the Polisario Front's 3rd Military District and its subordinate units in the 22,000km^2 patrol area around Mijek. This camp is the most inhospitable place in the sector, and it is very difficult to drive on the patrol routes due to the large amount of sand. Sahrawi soldiers have several observation points in the area. Apart from the district command, there are 10 companies in the 3rd Military District, and the units are located close to the camp.

There are 64 registered wells in the district, the water of most of them can only be consumed by animals. On several occasions, the patrols visit the smaller and larger tent camps in the area, where

Polisario soldiers near the Mijek team site. (János Besenyő collection)

mostly relatives of Sahrawi soldiers or Bedouins who sympathise with them live. Since the area was the scene of serious fighting on multiple occasions, the unexploded ordnance and mines planted here pose a real danger to both military observers and the civilian population. This district has seen problems between peacekeepers and Polisario Front militants. For example, on 9 October 1995, locals surrounded the camp with a group of 10 heavily armed Land Rovers, and although the situation was extremely tense, no conflict arose. Only after three days did the militants leave the vicinity of the military observers' camp. MINURSO leaders sent an official report on the incident to the UN's headquarters in New York. In the same month, the commander of the military district banned reconnaissance flights over his units, regulated in military conventions and accepted by Polisario Front leaders. The commander stated that if a helicopter took off and made a reconnaissance flight it would be shot down. Since then, cooperation in this district has not been without problems. The UN has developed five airports that are suitable for receiving helicopters and Antonovs.

Largely ignored in public is that MINURSO produces locust monitoring reports and keeps the Food and Agriculture Organization of the United Nations constantly updated on their migrations. This picture was taken near the Mijek team site, where a huge swarm of locusts grazed almost everything to the ground. (János Besenyő collection)

Tindouf

Independent of the sectors, the MINURSO liaison office at Tindouf operates under the headquarters and maintains contact with the refugee camps and the Polisario Front administrative centre in Rabouni.

The city is located approximately 1,400km from the capital of Algeria and serves as the headquarters of the Algerian Western Military District. The city hosts both land and air force units. During the 2000s, the air force deployed Soviet-made Mikoyan i Gurevich MiG-23 fighter-bombers there, and the ground units are mostly equipped with military equipment of the Soviet origin. The weapons of the Algerian troops stationed here, even if not the most modern, are in good condition, and their training and morale are very good. There are several military checkpoints in and around the city, where soldiers and the Algerian Gendarmerie check all passers-by very thoroughly. Due to the serious military presence, the Islamic fundamentalists could not gain ground.

The UN office operates under the close supervision of the Algerian authorities and the Polisario Front, which often makes work very difficult. Without a liaison officer, the military observers cannot move, and even with one they can only visit the refugee camps, the airport, and the town of Rabouni (Polisario centre). Visits to military units and taking photos of any military object is strictly prohibited. The military observers patrol an area of about 24,000km^2, but this area is not under the UN's control and so they

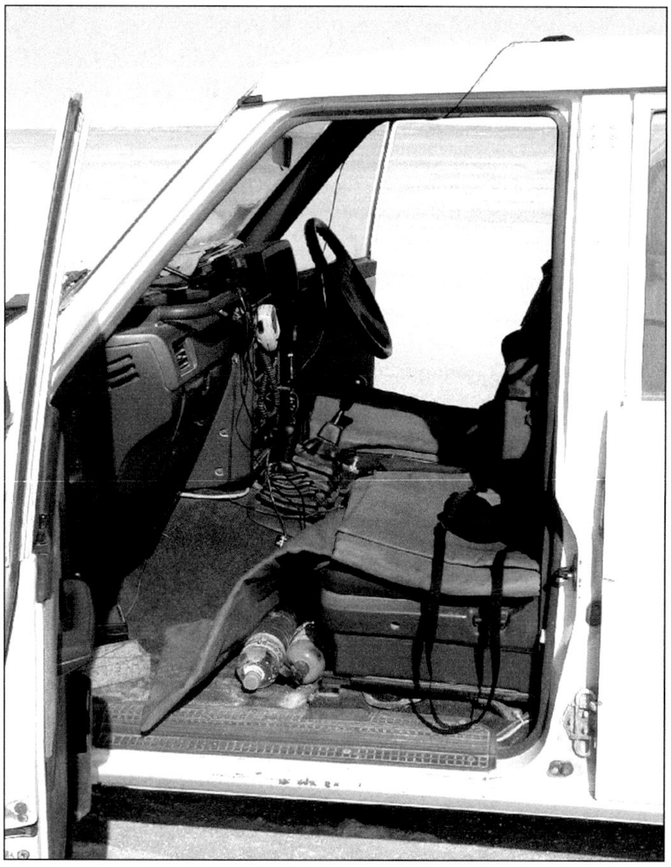

Peacekeepers try to reduce the danger posed by unexploded shells and mines by placing bulletproof vests and sandbags on the seats and the floor of patrol cars. These can reduce the effects of a possible explosion, thus increasing the peacekeepers' chance of survival. (János Besenyő collection)

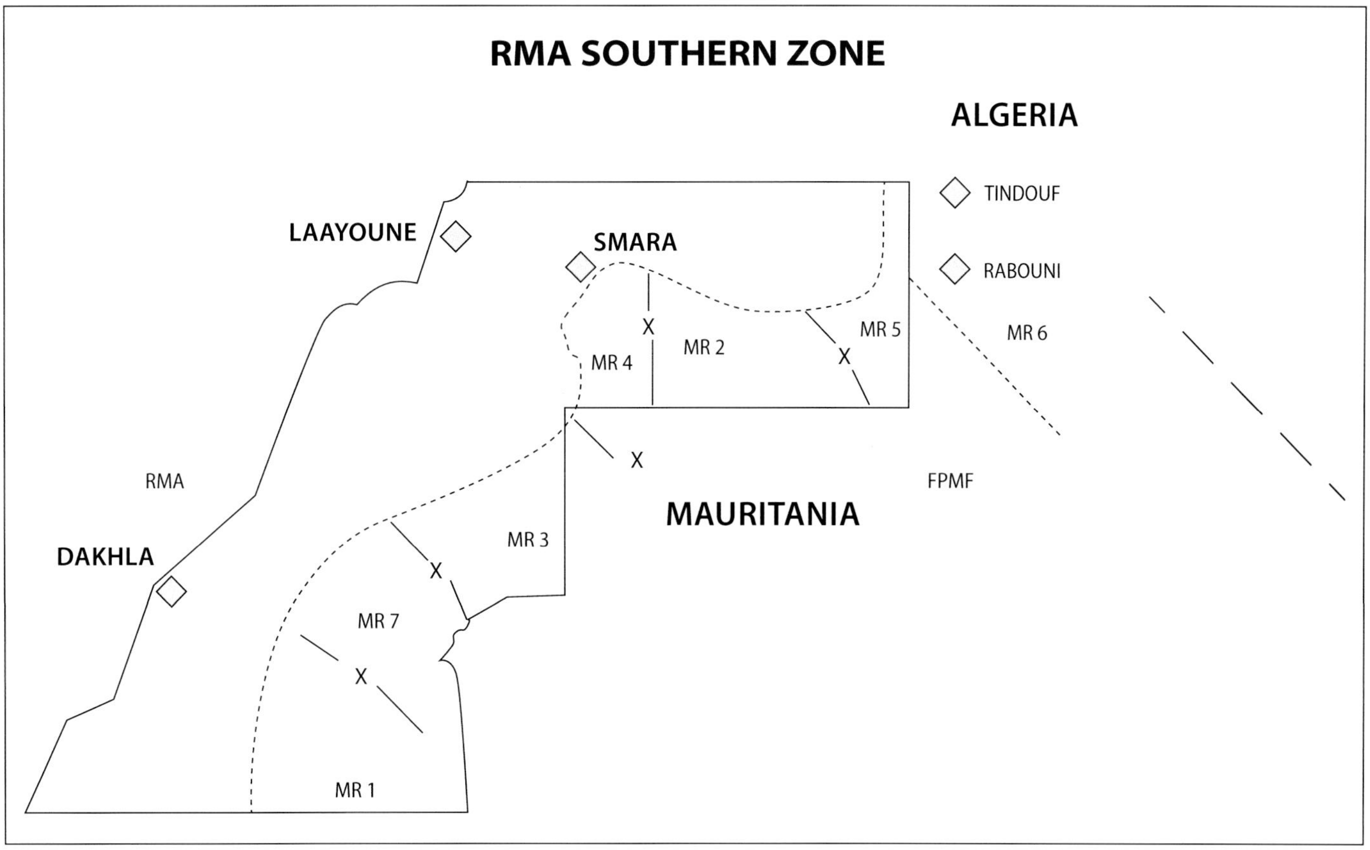

The Polisario Front military districts. (Diagram by author)

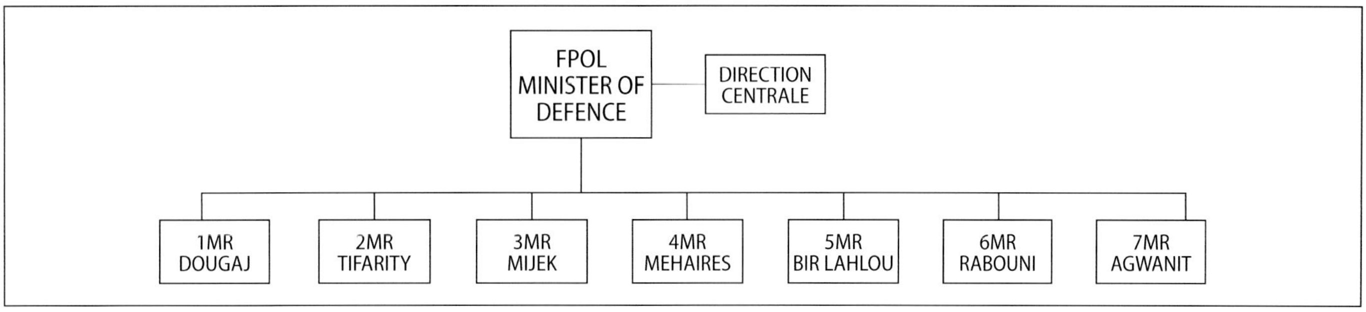

Organisation of the Polisario Front's military wing. (Diagram by author)

do not have the authority to take action, they can only report the results of their observations to the headquarters. Of course, the observers enjoy diplomatic protection, and there have been no clashes between the Algerian authorities and those serving here.

Located here are the 6th Military District and the Ministry of Defence of the Sahrawi Arab Democratic Republic (the Polisario Front headquarters). There are four military schools, four logistical and repair bases, a military hospital and a rehabilitation institute for soldiers injured during the fighting and those released from Moroccan captivity. The logistical bases created for the provision of supplies to the other districts also belong to the subordination of the district commander. It is almost impossible to obtain realistic information about this region, as the Polisario Front leaders are reluctant to give information to the UN for fear of it falling into the hands of the Moroccan army. At one point, the MINURSO commander asked if the mission could get any information about the district and headquarters, to which the defence minister replied that such information was not the concern of military observers.

Civilian Police (CIVPOL)

When the UN adopted Resolution No. 690 on the establishment of MINURSO (29 April 1991), it was clear that certain tasks could not be performed by military observers due to the lack of adequate training, so the UN Secretary-General proposed sending police forces to the mission. In his report (paragraph S/22464/46 – 19 April 1991), the Secretary-General initiated the immediate employment of 100 police officers to facilitate the work of those preparing the census. Later, they would have increased the number by another 200 people to ensure the return of the refugees to the territories occupied by Morocco. However, at the beginning of 1992, only the Uruguayan police general in charge of the police component of the mission was in the area of operations: the police unit he would have commanded existed only on paper.[64]

From the very beginning, the police force cooperated closely with the employees of the Identification Office, with whom joint work began in July 1993 under the leadership of police Colonel Jürgen Friedrich Reinman.[65] The first police unit consisted of 19 people (four Germans, five Belgians, five Malaysians, and five Togolese), who also provided security for the mission. However, their main task was to accompany and protect the employees of the

A joint military-police patrol of the Tindouf refugee camps in 2003. (János Besenyő collection)

MINURSO patrols inspect one of the emergency airports designated for the UN in the desert. (János Besenyő collection)

which played an active role in the mission's life for years with varying numbers.[71] On 25 March 1995, the following countries served in the 78-person police department: Austria (10), Germany (5), Hungary (13), Malaysia (15), Nigeria (15), Norway (5), Togo (5), and Uruguay (10). During the rest of the year, Togo sent another 11 policemen, while Ghana, which had just joined the mission, sent a police contingent of 15 people to Western Sahara, so the number reached 104 personnel. This number was still insufficient to fulfil the increased number of tasks, so the police Colonel Wolf-Dieter Krampe, who replaced the former police commander, requested the deployment of 99 more police officers from the UN. The Secretary-General promised to increase the size of police units as soon as possible, but this failed due to the lack of offers from the member states. In the same year one of the policemen was sent back to his country before the end of his service due to causing a road accident, a step usually only taken as a last resort in peace operations.[72] On 20 August 1995, Colonel Krampe, who led the police, left Western Sahara and was succeeded by the Norwegian police Lieutenant Colonel Jan Walman. During this period, the Hungarian police contingent was the second largest police unit in the

Identification Office during the preparation for the referendum.[66] As soon as the census of those entitled to vote began, the number of police officers increased proportionally with their duties, and by the end of the year, it had risen to 26 people.[67] In his March 1994 report, the UN Secretary-General authorised the employment of said 26 police officers,[68] and by the end of the year, 50 had already been commissioned.[69] At that time, the following countries sent police officers to the mission: Austria (10), Germany (5), Malaysia (15), Nigeria (5), Norway (5), Togo (5), and Uruguay (5). Although the Resolution (973/1995) of the Security Council dated 1995 allowed the size of police units to be increased from 55 to 160 people, this never happened, and in fact, another reduction in size followed and then another expansion again. At the end of 1995, the largest size of the police unit was 92 people.[70] The year 1995 is very important from the Hungarian point of view, because it was then that the 13-member Hungarian police contingent began its service in Western Sahara,

mission area.[73] In January 1996, Lieutenant Colonel Walman left the mission at the end of his service, and was succeeded by the Austrian police General Walter Fallman, who was also faced with the fact that he could not provide enough policemen for the activities of the Identification Office. Although he repeatedly requested an increase in the number of police officers, only 91 police officers still served in the mission.[74] The situation was complicated by the increasingly problematic cooperation between the opposing parties, which led to a reduction in the size of the mission, so that at the end of the summer, only 44 of the 91 police officers were in the operational area, of which the Hungarians had the largest contingent.[75]

At that time, 19 Identification Centres (IDCs) were established in Morocco, Mauritania, and Algeria, where the police were on duty along with civilian employees. The duties of the police included maintaining order and enforcing the law in the Identification Centres and ensuring the continuous and safe work

Lessons Learned from the Author's Personal Experiences

In this chapter, I have tried to gather as much information as possible, as this data can be of significant help to those who wish to deal with the region in more detail. I have also shared with the readers some of the stories that happened to the peacekeepers, and I also want to write about a very important thing about the mission that I have not talked about so far. As in so many places, especially where daily activities are limited by strict rules, during the MINURSO mission, the so-called natural laws and general rules, which have proven to be true, emerge from general experience. I would like to make some of these unwritten rules public:

- Never argue with the French
- Never drink with the Russians
- Flies have a low protein content and have a distinctly bad taste
- A straight line is not always the shortest path between two points
- A GPS error of 200 metres is not acceptable when you are looking for the location of a mine
- What happens during leave should stay there
- MINURSO's two most important words: CTO (leave) and MSA (salary)
- Nothing moves in the desert on a hot day except camels and UN observers
- If you have received your vaccinations, there is no food offered by the locals that you could not and should not eat
- The mafia no longer exists only among Italians (a reference to the fact that members of larger participating nations sometimes team up, for example: Latin Americans, Russians, French, Chinese, especially the language in common is the unifying force)
- This is not Hell yet, but you can already see it from here
- Scorpions and snakes are not in the 'cool' category when you turn on the lights and meet them in your room
- 'Professional' is a relative term
- The regulations are always right
- The regulations never work
- You are not rally driver Colin McRae
- Looking back at the 'minefield' sign may not be a good omen
- The day you forget to check if you have the jack is the day you have a flat tyre
- If something can break down, it will

of civilian employees.[76] The UN established identification offices in Laayoune, Dakhla, Boujdour, Smara, Tan-Tan, Goulimine, Assa, Rabat, Casablanca, Marakesh, Sidi Kacem, Zagora, Taroudant, Tata, Zourat, Nouadhibou, Elkelaa, Meknes, and Tindouf.

During the identification period, the main tasks of the police were as follows:

Members of the Hungarian Police Contingent at the mission headquarters, 1996. (János Besenyő collection)

- Ensure that everyone who wanted to take part in the referendum that will decide the future of the area was registered and given the opportunity to vote after presenting their authentic documents.
- Photographing and taking fingerprints of those entitled to vote to facilitate the identification of voters later.
- Escorting the leaders of the tribes and those persons who facilitated the work of the UN in the preparation of the census.
- Personal and facility protection tasks.
- Collecting the documents processed during the identification process, then transporting them to Tindouf and Laayoune, and finally delivering all the documents to the UN headquarters located in Genoa (346,000 documents were transported to Genoa by the end of December 2003).
- Escorting the paymasters delivering salaries to UN employees and military observers, and protecting payment locations.
- Organisation of joint patrol trips with military observers in the area of Laayoune and Tindouf.
- Participation in the training of military observers (desert driving and navigation-GPS training).
- Preparation of a plan for the establishment, training, and monitoring – in accordance with democratic standards – of the police forces of the autonomous Western Sahara.

- Assisting the work of the security service and carrying out other tasks requiring technical and police knowledge.
- Advising police and security policy issues to the military and civilian leadership of the mission.
- Participation in the refugee resettlement programme.
- Investigating disciplinary and other criminal matters involving MINURSO in cooperation with local authorities.
- Cooperation with the refugee office (UNHCR) in matters concerning refugees.

During the preparation period for the census, 81 police officers served in the territory of Western Sahara and the surrounding countries, which size was continuously reduced by the UN, so that at the end of 1996, only seven police officers (among them one Hungarian) were present in the mission, led by the Norwegian police Lieutenant Colonel Jan Cleven.[77] In 1997, the unit's staff consisted of only nine people, who mainly performed guard and security tasks in the mission.[78] The leadership of the mission then proposed the complete abolition of the police department.[79] In the end, the UN did not disband the police unit, but it did not replace the police officers whose term of service had expired, so in June 1997, the police force only existed nominally in the mission.[80] However, they were soon faced with a multitude of problems arising from the lack of police officers, so by the end of 1997, they had begun to fill up the police unit again.

By the beginning of 1998, 79 police officers from the following countries were serving in the MINURSO staff: Canada (5), Egypt (2), Ghana (10), India (10), Malaysia (10), Nigeria (10), Norway (2), Pakistan (10), Portugal (10), and Sweden (10). The new commander of the unit was the Canadian chief detective, Peter Miller.[81] The police mainly participated in the identification process and created an expert group that made plans and recommendations related to the conduct of the referendum. By the end of August 1998, the police unit had reached the size of 81 authorised by the UN.[82] At the beginning of 1999, Peter Miller left the mission, so the command of the police unit was taken over by Indian Lieutenant Colonel Sunil Roy, who soon had to face downsizing again. Then, the size of the contingent was 26 people. Of course, this caused a serious problem during daily work.[83] Based on the indications of the mission's leadership, the UN once again invited member countries to send police officers to Western Sahara, who responded positively to the request, so by the end of June 1999, the police unit consisted of 52 people. By the end of the year, the number of the contingent was again increased to 81 people. It was then that the Indian police General Om Prakash Rathor became the head of the unit, who managed the police work in the mission area until the end of 2003.[84]

In 2000, the police, in addition to continuing their classic police activities, mainly assisted the staff of the Identification Office and patrolled the operational area together with the soldiers. By the summer of 2000, the number of personnel had decreased again, and by the end of the year, only 26 police officers were serving in the mission. Since the identification process had been completed by then, the remaining police officers were stationed in the cities of Laayoune and Tindouf, where they mainly dealt with security and training tasks.[85] In the years to come, the number of police units remained permanently low, and their main activity was the preparation of UNHCR staff in connection with the resettlement of refugees. Of course, they continued to cooperate with the staff of the Identification Office and regularly carried out joint patrols with the members of the mission's military contingent. In 2003, the management of the mission – due to economic considerations – proposed to close the Identification Office and to reduce the number of personnel on the mission, which affected the police contingent that had been operating with only 14 people by then.[86] Thus, the police unit was completely abolished at the end of December due to the conclusion of the identification process and the indefinite suspension of the work of the Identification Office.[87]

However, it soon became clear that the work of the police was needed, so in 2005, a group of six police officers started working again in the MINURSO staff.[88] During the past years, the discipline of the police unit operating in the mission was excellent, only two police officers had to be sent back to their country before the end of their service, one due to causing a road accident and one due to the insufficient knowledge of the English language.[89] In 2022, the number of police officers was reduced to two.[90]

Conclusion

The organisational structure of MINURSO is complex, but it is necessary for a disciplined and well-ordered operation. The high command manages the mission effectively, and the operation and structure of the subordinate departments operating at the headquarters is also logical and well organised. Each area has its own person in charge who brings the individual departments together, and then, in turn, they are managed by the headquarters. The orderly and lawful operation of the mission is supervised by the UN Secretary-General's Special Envoy, who is ultimately responsible to the leadership of the UN. The various camp tasks are distributed proportionately, everyone receives preliminary training, knows his place, and is able to perform his tasks at a high level. The situation is similar at lower levels as well as the team sites, where the less-in-numbers but more dedicated soldiers have to cope with the difficulties caused by nature and the opposing parties. It is not always easy for individual smaller units to supervise the vast areas entrusted to them, but practice and the history of MINURSO so far show that they are able to control extremely large areas even with a small number of personnel. All in all, it can be said that the structure of MINURSO's military and civilian system shows surprising efficiency and organisation, which is why the work there continues quite smoothly and without major interruptions to this day.

Bibliography

Archival Sources (UN Documents)

A/HRC/49/4, Report of the Independent Fact-Finding Mission on Libya, UN Human Rights Council, 23 March 2022

S/1994/1257, The situation concerning Western Sahara-report by the Secretary-General, 5 November 1994

S/1994/283, The situation concerning Western Sahara-report by the Secretary-General, 23 March 1994

S/1994/819, The situation concerning Western Sahara-report by the Secretary-General, 12 July 1994

S/1995/240, The situation concerning Western Sahara-report by the Secretary-General, 30 March 1995

S/1995/404, The situation concerning Western Sahara-report by the Secretary-General, 19 May 1995

S/1995/779, The situation concerning Western Sahara-report by the Secretary-General, 8 September 1995

S/1996/43, Report of the Secretary-General on the Situation Concerning Western Sahara, 19 January 1996

S/1996/343, Report of the Secretary-General on the Situation Concerning Western Sahara, 8 May 1996

S/1996/674, Progress Report of the Secretary-General on the Situation Concerning Western Sahara, 20 August 1996

S/1996/913, Report of the Secretary-General on the Situation Concerning Western Sahara, 5 November 1996

S/1997/166, Letter Dated 10 March 1997 from the Permanent Representative of Morocco to the United Nations Addressed to the President of the Security Council, 10 March 1997

S/1997/358, Report of the Secretary-General on the Situation Concerning Western Sahara, 5 May 1997

S/1997/742, Report of the Secretary-General on the Situation Concerning Western Sahara, 24 September 1997

S/1998/35, Report of the Secretary-General on the Situation Concerning Western Sahara, 15 January 1998

S/1998/775, Progress Report of the Secretary-General on the Situation Concerning Western Sahara, 18 August 1998

S/1999/307, Report of the Secretary-General on the Situation Concerning Western Sahara, 22 March 1999

S/1999/1219, Report of the Secretary-General on the Situation Concerning Western Sahara, 6 December 1999

S/2000/1029, Report of the Secretary-General on the Situation Concerning Western Sahara, 25 October 2000

S/2000/461, Report of the Secretary-General on the situation concerning Western Sahara, 22 May 2000

S/2001/613, Report of the Secretary-General on the situation concerning Western Sahara, 20 June 2001

S/2002/41, Interim report of the Secretary-General on the situation concerning Western Sahara, 10 January 2002

S/2003/565, Report of the Secretary-General on the situation concerning Western Sahara, 23 May 2003

S/2003/1016, Report of the Secretary-General on the Situation Concerning Western Sahara, 16 October 2003

S/2004/39, Report of the Secretary-General on the Situation Concerning Western Sahara, 19 January 2004

S/2005/254, Report of the Secretary-General on the Situation Concerning Western Sahara, 19 April 2005

S/2005/648, Report of the Secretary-General on the situation concerning Western Sahara, 13 October 2005

S/2006/817, Report of the Secretary-General on the situation concerning Western Sahara, 16 October 2006

S/2010/175, Report of the Secretary-General on the situation concerning Western Sahara, 6 April 2010

S/2011/249, Report of the Secretary-General on the situation concerning Western Sahara, 1 April 2011

S/2017/307, Report of the Secretary-General on the situation concerning Western Sahara, 10 April 2017

S/2018/277, Report of the Secretary-General on the situation concerning Western Sahara, 29 March 2018

S/2018/889, Report of the Secretary-General on the situation concerning Western Sahara, 3 October 2018

S/2019/282, Report of the Secretary-General on the situation concerning Western Sahara, 1 April 2019

S/2019/787, Report of the Secretary-General on the situation concerning Western Sahara, 2 October 2019

S/2020/938, The situation concerning Western Sahara-report by the Secretary-General, 23 September 2020

S/2021/843, The situation concerning Western Sahara-report by the Secretary-General, 01 October 2021

S/22464, The situation concerning Western Sahara-report by the Secretary-General, 19 April 1991

S/23662, Report of the Secretary-General on the United Nations Mission for the Referendum in Western Sahara, 28 February 1992

S/24040, The situation concerning Western Sahara-report by the Secretary-General, 29 May 1992

S/24464, Letter Dated 31 August 1992 from the President of the Security Council Addressed to the Secretary-General, 31 August 1992

S/25170, The situation concerning Western Sahara-report by the Secretary-General, 26 January 1993

S/26797, The situation concerning Western Sahara-report by the Secretary-General, 24 November 1993

S/RES/2602, Resolution 2602, 29 October 2021

Online Sources

Alaoui, Mohamed 'Tensions rise with Morocco as Russia receives Polisario delegation', *The Arab Weekly*, 23 October 2021, https://thearabweekly.com/tensions-rise-morocco-russia-receives-polisario-delegation, accessed 19 May 2022

Anon., 'After 12 years, Korean medical unit departs UN mission in Western Sahara', *UN News*, 15 May 2006, https://news.un.org/en/story/2006/05/178832-after-12-years-korean-medical-unit-departs-un-mission-western-sahara, accessed 28 June 2022)

Anon., *Akhbar Es-Sahra (News of The Sahara), Western Sahara Mission UK & Ireland*, Newsletter N°2, 10 January 2002, http://www.arso.org/akhbar2.htm, accessed 28 June 2022

Anon., *Ceasefire monitoring, MINURSO homepage*, https://minurso.unmissions.org/ceasefire-monitoring, accessed 28 June 2022

Anon., *Foro de Inteligencia, Espionaje y Servicios Secretos Foro sobre: Inteligencia, Espionaje y Servicios Secretos*, http://www.intelpage.info/forum/viewtopic.php?t=132, accessed 19 May 2022

Anon., 'How the War in Ukraine May Impact Africa', *Center for Strategic & International Studies*, 1 March 2022, https://www.csis.org/analysis/how-war-ukraine-may-impact-africa, accessed 20 May 2022

Anon., *January 2019 Monthly Forecast, Security Council Report*, 27 December 2018, https://www.securitycouncilreport.org/monthly-forecast/2019-01/western-sahara.php, accessed 19 May 2022

Anon., *Mine action, MINURSO homepage*, https://minurso.unmissions.org/mine-action, accessed 28 June 2022

Anon., *MINURSO fact sheet, MINURSO homepage*, https://peacekeeping.un.org/en/mission/minurso, accessed 28 June 2022

Anon., 'MINURSO farewell Malaysian Medical Unit, welcome Bangladeshi Medical Unit', *MINURSO homepage*, 15 December 2010, https://minurso.unmissions.org/minurso-farewell-malaysian-medical-unit-welcome-bangladeshi-medical-unit, accessed 28 June 2022

Anon., 'MINURSO: Testimonio de una mujer de Montenegro', *Maghreb online*, 10 July 2021, https://moroccomail.fr/2021/10/07/minurso-testimonio-de-una-mujer-de-montenegro/, accessed 19 May 2022

Anon., 'MINURSO The United Nations Mission for the Referendum in Western Sahara: Der Weg zum VN-Militärbeobachter – Teil 3', Mahbas, 16 October 2020, https://www.bundeswehr.de/de/einsaetze-bundeswehr/die-bundeswehr-in-marokko/einsatz-minurso-vn-militaebeobachter-westsahara-3555412, accessed 28 June 2022

Anon., 'Morocco scents victory in Western Sahara', *The Economist*, 26 March 2022, https://www.economist.com/middle-east-and-africa/2022/03/26/morocco-scents-victory-in-western-sahara, accessed 20 May 2022

Anon., 'New developments around Western Sahara could create an opportunity for Africa to assert its position', *ISS, PSC Report*, 03 June 2016, https://issafrica.org/pscreport/psc-insights/a-new-opportunity-to-assert-africas-role-in-western-sahara, accessed 19 May 2022

Anon., *Office Locations, MINURSO homepage*, https://minurso.unmissions.org/office-locations, accessed 28 June 2022

Anon., 'Paris-Dakar Rally Driver Hits Land Mine', *ABC News*, 8 January 2001, http://abcnews.go.com/International/story?id=81746&page=1, accessed 28 June 2022

Anon., *Review of Aviation Safety in the Department of Peacekeeping Operations, United Nations Archives*, https://search.archives.un.org/uploads/r/united-nations-archives /d/7/6/d765b92a3231ea25aba82ddf7aa83a5d681 b0adf1ec152c95fc186fffee35b00/S-1092-0102-06-00012.pdf, accessed 28 June 2022

Anon., *skyscrapercity.com/Moroccan Air Armed Forces*, http://www.skyscrapercity.com/showthread.php?t=442085, accessed 19 May 2022

Anon., 'Things are heating up in Western Sahara', *The Economist*, 6 November 2021, https://www.economist.com/middle-east-and-africa/2021/11/06/things-are-heating-up-in-western-sahara, accessed 18 May 2022

Anon., 'Time for International Re-engagement in Western Sahara', *International Crisis Group*, Briefeing no. 82, 11 March 2021, https://www.crisisgroup.org/middle-east-north-africa/north-africa/western-sahara/b82-time-international-re-engagement-western-sahara, accessed at: 16 May 2022

Anon., *Troop and police contributors, MINURSO homepage*, https://peacekeeping.un.org/en/troop-and-police-contributors, accessed 28 June 2022

Anon., 'Un Descendant au Sahara Occidental, par le capitane Michel Barbaize', *La Kouma, 42' ANNÉE, No. 157* (2000), https://lakoumia.fr/images/bulletins/LA%20KOUMIA%20numero%20157.pdf, accessed 19 May 2022

Anon., 'Western Sahara', *Security Council Report*, 31 March 2022, https://www.securitycouncilreport.org/monthly-forecast/2022-04/western-sahara-8.php, accessed 18 May 2022

Anon., *World Peace Foundation: Western Sahara Short Mission Brief*, July 2017, https://sites.tufts.edu/wpf/files/2017/07/Western-Sahara-brief.pdf, accessed 16 May 2022

Anon., 'YO FUI CASCO AZUL EN EL SAHARA (por el Comodoro VGM (R) Carlos Fernando VIÑAS)', February 2021,https://aevyca.com.ar/wp-content/uploads/2021/02/Yo-fui-Casco-Azul-en-el-Sahara.pdf, accessed 18 May 2022

Besenyő, János, 'The role of the Spanish Legion in the Spanish possessions of Ifni, Tarfaya and West Sahara', *Revista Digital de Historia Militar*, 15 July 2020, https://historiamilitar.es/the-role-of-the-spanish-legion-in-the-spanish-possessions-of-ifni-tarfaya-and-west-sahara/?fbclid=IwAR1-kEALBT65hDyxbenRlpRC9B6yiDi1VtUqtpwnCvNb22W7ye4agSr6jvw, accessed 19 May 2022

Boukhars, Anouar, 'The drivers of insecurity in Mauritania', *The Carnegie Papers*, April 2012,https://carnegieendowment.org/files/mauritania_insecurity.pdf, accessed 28 June 2022

Davies, Sara E., Rushton, Simon, 'Healing or Harming? United Nations Peacekeeping and Health' (New York: International Peace Institute, March 2015) https://www.ipinst.org/wp-content/uploads/2015/03/IPI_Rpt_Health_and_Peacekeeping.pdf, accessed 28 June 2022

Dworkin, Anthony, 'North AFrican standoff: How the Western Sahara conflict is fuelling new tensions between Morocco and Algeria', *European Council on Foreign Relations*, 8 April 2022, https://ecfr.eu/publication/north-african-standoff-how-the-western-sahara-conflict-is-fuelling-new-tensions-between-morocco-and-algeria/, accessed 18 May 2022

Fabricius, Peter, 'Ukraine War reveals Africa divided', *Institute for Security Studies*, 18 March 2022, https://issafrica.org/iss-today/ukraine-war-reveals-africa-divided, accessed 20 May 2022

Gallagher, Conor, 'Last two Irish troops withdraw from Western Sahara after 30 years. Defence Forces leave at precarious time for United Nations Minurso mission', *The Irish Times*, 29 July 2021, https://www.irishtimes.com/news/ireland/irish-news/last-two-irish-troops-withdraw-from-western-sahara-after-30-years-1.4633766, accessed 19 May 2022

Grinblat, Joseph Alfred, 'My Work on the Origins of Minurso, the UN Mission in Western Sahara', 27 October 2021, https://www.passblue.com/2021/10/27/my-work-on-the-origins-of-minurso-the-un-mission-in-western-sahara/, accessed 18 May 2022

Hill, Thomas M., 'Ukraine War Puts New Focus on Conflict in Western Sahara', *United States Institute of Peace*, 14 April 2022, https://www.usip.org/publications/2022/04/ukraine-war-puts-new-focus-conflict-western-sahara, accessed 20 May 2022

Huddleston, R. Joseph, 'Can John Bolton Thaw Western Sahara's Long-Frozen Conflict?', *Foreign Policy*, 9 May 2019, https://foreignpolicy.com/2019/05/09/can-john-bolton-thaw-western-saharas-long-frozen-conflict-morocco-western-sahara-polisario-minurso-sahrawi-republic/, accessed 16 May 2022

Jay, Martin, 'Blinken's Slick "Diplo Talk" Can't Fix Algeria-Morocco Rift', *Inside Arabia*, 11 April 2022, https://insidearabia.com/blinkens-slick-diplo-talk-cant-fix-algeria-morocco-rift/, accessed 20 May 2022

Lee, Matthew, 'Blinken urges Algria re-think on Russia, Western Sahara', *AP News*, 30 March 2022, https://apnews.com/article/russia-ukraine-middle-east-africa-antony-blinken-north-africa-f3d4b0be50608327e8cdcc1057bebfe9, accessed 20 May 2022

Michael, Dibie Ike, 'UN mission in Western Sahara renewed for only six months', *Africanews*, 01 November 2018, https://www.africanews.com/2018/11/01/un-mission-in-western-sahara-renewed-for-only-six-months/, accessed 19 May 2022

Mohsen-Finan, Khadija, 'Morocco's indignation with Ban Ki-moon: is the Western Sahara an 'occupied' territory?', *Real Instituto Elcano*, 26 July 2016, https://www.realinstitutoelcano.org/en/analyses/moroccos-indignation-with-ban-ki-moon-is-the-western-sahara-an-occupied-territory/, accessed 19 May 2022

Pack, Jason, 'Libya's Chaos Is a Warning to the World', *Foreign Policy*, 26 October 2021, https://foreignpolicy.com/2021/10/26/libya-chaos-qaddafi-turkey-uae-france-italy-russia-disorder/, accessed 18 May 2022

Paget, Sharif, McCluskey, Mitchell, 'Western Sahara independence leader declares the end of a 29-year-old ceasefire with Morocco', *CNN.com*, 15 November 2020, https://edition.cnn.com/2020/11/15/world/polisario-front-morocco-western-sahara-ceasefire-intl/index.html, accessed 19 May 2022

Pinto, Teresa Nogueira, 'The fight goes on over Western Sahara's status', *GIS reports online*, 16 May 2022, https://www.gisreportsonline.com/r/western-sahara/, accessed 18 May 2022

Rogers, Philippe D., 'China and United Nations Peacekeeping Operations in Africa', *Naval War College Review*, vol. 60, issue 2, article 7 (2007), https://digital-commons.usnwc.edu/nwc-review/vol60/iss2/7, accessed 19 May 2022

Rousselier, Jacques, 'A Role for Russia in the Western Sahara?', *Carnegie Endowment for International Peace*, 05 June 2018, https://carnegieendowment.org/sada/76532, accessed 19 May 2022

Royal Moroccan Army – Order of Battle, GlobalSecurity.org, https://www.globalsecurity.org/military/world/morocco/army-orbat.htm accessed 28 June 2022

Saleh, Heba, 'Algeria and Morocoo fall out over gas, separatists and Western Sahara', *Financial Times*, 18 October 2021, https://www.ft.com/content/7b21472a-9ffb-44ae-846a-6cc85e228ca6, accessed 18 May 2022

Salem, Zekeria Ould Ahmed, 'Rethinking the weak state paradigm in light of the war on terror: Evidence from the Islamic Republic of Mauritania', *The Project on Middle East Political Science (POMEPS)*, https://pomeps.org/rethinking-the-weak-state-paradigm-in-light-of-the-war-on-terror-evidence-from-the-islamic-republic-of-mauritania, accessed 28 June 2022

Sanderson, Sertan, 'Western Sahara: A migrant smuggling hotspot', *Info Migrants*, 22 January 2021, https://www.infomigrants.net/en/post/29818/western-sahara-a-migrant-smuggling-hotspot, accessed 19 May 2022

Shihao, Cai, Ying, Liang and Beiping, Tai, 'Surviving in the sand', *China Daily*, 21 December 2007, https://www.chinadaily.com.cn/cndy/2007-12/21/content_6337521.htm, accessed 18 May 2022

Souaré, Issaka K., 'Western Sahara. Is there light at the end of the tunnel?', *ISS Paper 155*, November 2007, https://www.files.ethz.ch/isn/98919/OP155.pdf, accessed 19 May 2022

Száraz, György, 'UN mission in Western Sahara (MINURSO)', in Dr. Gömbös, Ervin (ed.), *The future of development policies and changing priorities: Africa*, (United Nations Association of Hungary, HUNIDA Kht, 2006) http://menszt.hu/data/file/Publication20060630.pdf accessed 18 May 2022

Tanchum, Michäel, 'The post-COVID-19 Trajectory for Algeria, Morocco and Western Sahara', *Institutio Affari Internazionali*, 16 January 2021, https://www.iai.it/en/pubblicazioni/post-covid-19-trajectory-algeria-morocco-and-western-sahara, accessed 20 May 2022

Theofilopoulou, Anna, 'The United Nations and Western Sahara. A Never-ending Affair', *United States Institute of Peace, Special Report*, July 2006, http://www.usip.org/files/resources/sr166.pdf, accessed 18 May 2022

Yago Rodrigues, The Armoured Force of the Moroccan Army, Ejercitos, 29/09/2018, https://www.revistaejercitos.com/en/2018/09/29/the-armored-force-of-the-morocco-army/ accessed 28 June 2022

Monographs and Articles

Azimi, Nassrine, *The Role and Functions of the Civilian Police in the United Nations Peace-keeping Operations* (The Hague: Kluwer Law International, 1996)

Besenyő, János, 'Another Showdown in Western Sahara?', *Terrorism and Political Violence*, vol. 33, issue 3 (2021), pp. 649–656

Besenyő, János, *A nyugat-szaharai válság. Egy Magyar békefenntartó szemével* (Pécs: IDResearch Kft/Publikon Kiadó, 2012)

Besenyő, János, *Magyar békefenntartók Afrikában* (Budapest: Katonai Nemzetbiztonsági Szolgálat kiadványa, 2013)

Besenyő, János, *Western Sahara* (Pécs: Publikon Publishers, 2009)

Besenyő, János, 'Western-Sahara under the Spanish empire', *AARMS*, vol. 9, issue 2 (2010), pp. 195–215

Besenyő, János, and Miletics, Péter, *Országismertető. Marokkó és Nyugat-Szahara* (Budapest: Honvéd Vezérkar Tudományos Kutatóhely, a Katonai Nemzetbiztonsági Szolgálat és a Magyar Honvédség Geoinformációs Szolgálat kiadványa, 2017)

Besenyő, János, Fülöp, Sándor. 'Hand-made Austro-Hungarian Maps of the Rio de Oro Coast', *Journal of Central and Eastern European African Studies*, Vol. 1 No. 4 (2021), pp. 138-155

Chopra, Jarat, 'A Chance for Peace in Western Sahara', *Survival*, vol. 39, issue 3 (1997), pp. 51–65

Clough, Neil, *Western Saharan Conflict: Prolonged Conflict and Prospects for the Future* (thesis, Alabama, Air Command and Staff College, Air University, 2008)

Cordesman, Anthony H., *A Tragedy of Arms, Military and Security Developments in the Maghreb* (Westport, Conn.: Praeger, 2002)

Cordesman, Anthony H., Burke, Arleigh A. and Nerguizian, Aram, *The North African military balance: Force Developments & Regional Challenges*, (CSIS, 7 December 2010)

Cordesman, Anthony H., Nerguizian, Aram, *The North African military balance: force development in the Maghreb* (Washington D.C.: CSIS Press, 2009)

Damis, John, *Conflicts in Northwest Africa, The Western Sahara dispute* (Stanford: Hoover Institution Press, 1983)

Darbouche, Hakim, Zoubir, Yahia H., 'Conflicting International Policies and the Western Sahara Stalemate', *The International Spectator*, vol. 43, issue 1 (2008), pp. 91–105

de Barros, José Maria Sydow, 'Western Sahara: History, UN acting and foreign interests', *Brazilian Journal of African Studies*, vol. 5, issue 10. (July/December 2020), pp. 103-126

De Cuellar, Javier Pérez, *Pilgrimage for peace: a Secretary-General's memoir* (New York: St. Martin's Press, 1997)

Dunbar, Charles, 'Saharan Stasis: Status and Future Prospects of the Western Sahara Conflict', *Middle East Journal*, vol. 54, issue 4 (2000), pp. 522–545

Durch, William J. (ed.), *The Evolution of UN Peacekeeping, Case Studies, and Comparative Analysis* (New York: St. Martin's Press, 1993)

Ferreira, Sylvio de Souza, 'A experiência de observador militar da ONU no Saara Ocidental', *Conjuntura Austral*, vol. 8, issue 39-40 (dez. 2016/mar. 2017), pp. 24–43

Gordon, Ian Campell., 'Australians in Western Sahara', *Australian Defence Forces Journal*, issue 104 (January/February 1994), pp.83–86. and Felsche, Major Susan Lee, *Royal Australian Army Medical Corps*, Canberra Doctor (September 2017)

Hodges, Tony, *Western Sahara. The Roots of a Desert War* (Westport, Connecticut: Larence Hill & Company, 1983)

James, N. F., 'Brief History of Australian peacekeeping', *Australian Defence Forces Journal*, issue 104, (January/February 1994), pp. 3–18

Jett, Dennis C., *Why Peacekeeping Fails*, 20th Anniversary Edition (Palgrave Macmillan, 2019)

Jensen, Erik, *Western Sahara. Anatomy of a Stalemate?* (Colorado: Lynne Rienner Publishers, Inc. 2012)

Jensen, Geoffrey. War and Insurgency in the Western Sahara (Carlisle Barracks, PA: US Army War College, 2013)

Lawless, Richard, Monahan, Leila, *War and refugees: The Western Sahara conflict*, (London: Pinter Publishers, 1987)

Lewis, William H., *Military implications of United Nations peacekeeping operations* (Washington D. C: The Institute for National Strategic Studies, June 1993)

Macqueen, Norrie, *United Nations peacekeeping in Africa since 1960* (London: Routledge, Taylor and Francis, 2014)

Martínez-Milán, Jesús, Castañeda, Claudia Barona, *Western Sahara, Reasons for Extemporaneous Colonization and Decolonization, 1885–1975* (New York: Nova Science Publishers, 2021)

Mercer, John, *Spanish Sahara* (London: George Allen & Unwin Ltd., 1976)

Mundy, Jacob A., '"Seized of the Matter": The UN and the Western Sahara Dispute', *Mediterranean Quaterly*, vol. 15, issue 3 (2004), pp. 130–148

Norris, Harry Thirlwall, *The Arab conquest of the Western Sahara*, (London, New York and Beirut: Harlow, Longman, Librairie du Liban, 1986)

Outram-Leman, S., Scott, Alexander, 'Constructing a Legitimate Geography of the Sahara from a Captivity Narrative, 1821', *History in Africa*, Volume 43 (2016), pp. 63–94

Pabs, Martin, 'The Western Sahara conflict', *Scientia Militaria, South African Journal of Military Studies*, Volume 29 (1999), pp. 71–79

Pickart, George A., *The Western Sahara: The Referendum Process in Danger: A Staff Report to the Committee on Foreign Relations of the United States Senate*, United States. (Congress. Senate. Committee on Foreign Relations, 1992)

Price, David Lynn, *The Western Sahara* (London, Sage Publications, 1979)

Rézette, Robert, *The Western Sahara and the frontiers of Morocco* (Paris: Nouvelles Éditions Latines, 1975)

San Martín, Pablo, *Western Sahara: The Refugee Nation* (Cardiff: University of Wales Press, 2010)

Shelley, Toby, *Endgame in the Western Sahara: What Future for Africa's Last Colony* (London, New York: Zed Books, 2004)

Sismanidis, Roxane D. V., *Police Functions in Peace Operation, Report from Workshop organised by the United States Institute of Peace* (Washington D.C., United States Institute of Peace, 1997)

Spracher, William C., 'Seeking Cultural Intelligence in the Desert's Shifting Sands While Keeping Peace Along the Berm', *American Intelligence Journal*, vol. 30, issue 1 (2012), pp.105-115

Szmolka, Immaculada, *Western Sahara and the Arab Spring*, in: Ojeda-Garcia, Raquel, Fernández-Molina, Irene, Veguilla, Victoria, *Global, regional and local dimensions of Western Sahara's protracted decolonisation* (Palgrave Macmillan, 2017)

The Center on International Cooperation: Global Peace Operations, ANNUAL REVIEW OF 2006 (Lynne Rienner Publishers, 2006)

Theofilopoulou, Anna, *The United Nations' change in approach to resolving the Western Sahara conflict since the turn of the twenty-first century*, in Ojeda-Garcia, Raquel, Fernández-Molina, Irene, Veguilla, Victoria (eds.), *Global, regional and local dimensions of Western Sahara's protracted decolonisation* (Palgrave Macmillan, 2017)

Thompson, Virginia, Adloff, Richard, *The Western Saharans* (London: Barnes & Nobles, 1980)

Zoubir, Yahia H., Benabdallah-Gambier, Karima, 'The United States and the North African Imbroglio: Balancing Interests in Algeria, Morocco, and the Western Sahara', *Mediterranean Politics*, vol. 10, issue 2 (2005), pp.181–202

Zunes, Stephen, Mundy, Jacob, *Western Sahara – War, Nationalism and Conflict Irresolution* (New York: Syracuse University Press, 2010)

Zunes, Stephen, Mundy, Jacob, *Western Sahara: War, Nationalism, and Conflict Irresolution* (Second Edition, Syracuse Studies on Peace and Conflict Resolution, 2022)

NOTES

Introduction

1 The reader is directed to Helion's two volume *Showdown in Western Sahara* mini-series within the Africa@War series for a comprehensive military history of the twentieth century conflict in the region.

Chapter 1

1 John Mercer, *Spanish Sahara* (London: George Allen & Unwin Ltd., 1976), p. 23.
2 János Besenyő, *Western Sahara* (Pécs: Publikon Publishers, 2009), pp. 9–14; John Damis, *Conflicts in Northwest Africa, The Western Sahara Dispute* (Stanford: Hoover Institution Press, 1983), pp. 1–4.
3 Mercer, pp. 49–56.
4 Erik Jensen, *Western Sahara. Anatomy of a Stalemate?* (Colorado: Lynne Rienner Publishers, Inc. 2012), p. 21.
5 Tony Hodges, *Western Sahara. The Roots of a Desert War* (Westport, Connecticut: Larence Hill & Company, 1983), p. 3.
6 Besenyő (2009), p. 37.
7 Mercer, p. 66.
8 Mercer, pp. 70–71.
9 Robert Rézette, *The Western Sahara and the Frontiers of Morocco* (Paris: Nouvelles Éditions Latines, 1975), p. 37.
10 Stephen Zunes, Jacob Mundy, *Western Sahara: War, Nationalism, and Conflict Irresolution* (Second Edition, Syracuse Studies on Peace and *Conflict* Resolution, 2022), p. 96; Hodges, pp. 4–7.
11 Harry Thirlwall Norris, *The Arab Conquest of the Western Sahara* (London, New York and Beirut: Harlow, Longman, Librairie du Liban, 1986), pp. 28–29 and 173–174; Hodges, pp. 8–9; Jesús Martínez-Milán, Claudia Barona Castañeda, *Western Sahara, Reasons for Extemporaneous Colonization and Decolonization, 1885–1975* (New York: Nova Science Publishers, 2021), pp. 4–9.
12 Mercer, pp. 76–77.
13 Rézette, pp. 51–52; Besenyő (2009), p. 45.
14 János Besenyő, 'Western-Sahara under the Spanish empire', *AARMS*, vol. 9, issue 2 (2010), pp. 195–215; Hodges, pp. 17–18.
15 Mercer, pp. 78–80.

16 János Besenyő, 'Another Showdown in Western Sahara?', *Terrorism and Political Violence*, vol. 33, issue 3 (2021), pp. 649–656.
17 Hodges, pp. 20–22.
18 Besenyő (2009), p. 47.
19 Mercer, p. 89.
20 Martínez-Milán, Castañeda, pp. 26–27; Hodges, pp. 25–36.
21 Mercer, pp. 91–99.
22 S. Outram-Leman, Alexander Scott, 'Constructing a Legitimate Geography of the Sahara from a Captivity Narrative, 1821', *History in Africa*, Volume 43 (2016), pp. 43 and 63–94.
23 Martínez-Milán, Castañeda, pp. 23–24.
24 Virginia, Thompson, Richard Adloff, *The Western Saharans* (London: Barnes & Nobles, 1980), pp. 104–105; Besenyő (2009), pp. 49–50; Rézette: pp. 61–72.
25 János Besenyő, Sándor Fülöp. 'Hand-made Austro-Hungarian Maps of the Rio de Oro Coast', *Journal of Central and Eastern European African Studies*, Vol. 1 No. 4 (2021), pp. 138–155, https://jceeas.bdi.uni-obuda.hu/index.php/jceeas/article/view/70/36 accessed 11 Sept 2022.
26 Zunes, Mundy, p. 99.
27 Mercer, pp. 110–116.; Jensen, Geoffrey. *War and Insurgency in the Western Sahara* (Carlisle Barracks, PA: US Army War College, 2013), p. 6.
28 Pablo San Martín, *Western Sahara: The Refugee Nation* (Cardiff: University of Wales Press, 2010), pp. 20–35.
29 Jensen, pp. 12–13.
30 Besenyő (2009), pp. 57–61; Thompson, Adloff, pp. 106–107; Rézette, p. 101.
31 San Martín, pp. 66–69; Martínez-Milán, Castañeda, pp. 95–114.
32 Zunes, Mundy, p. 102.
33 Ifni was never recovered by the Spanish and thus the Moroccans would reclaim it in 1969. János Besenyő, 'The role of the Spanish Legion in the Spanish possessions of Ifni, Tarfaya and West Sahara', *Revista Digital de Historia Militar*, 15 July 2020, https://historiamilitar.es/the-role-of-the-spanish-legion-in-the-spanish-possessions-of-ifni-tarfaya-and-west-sahara/?fbclid=IwAR1-kEALBT65hDyxbenRlpRC9B6yiDi1VtUqtpwnCvNb22W7ye4agSr6jvw, accessed 19 May 2022.
34 Hodges, pp. 73–83; San Martín, p. 70.
35 Richard Lawless, Leila Monahan, *War and Refugees: The Western Sahara Conflict* (London: Pinter Publishers, 1987), pp. 48–50; Besenyő (2009), p. 65; San Martín, pp. 74–81.; Martínez-Milán, Castañeda, pp. 83–87.
36 David Lynn Price, *The Western Sahara* (London, Sage Publications, 1979), p. 14; Mercer, pp. 228–229; Thompson, Adloff, pp. 137–138.
37 Hodges, pp. 85–88; Damis, pp. 15–25.
38 Besenyő (2009), pp. 65–67; Thompson, Adloff, pp. 139–143; Price, pp. 27–35.
39 Lawless, Monahan, pp. 9–15.
40 Jensen, pp. 25–27; Besenyő (2009), pp. 73–75.
41 Mercer, pp. 240–243; Zunes, Mundy, p. 105.; Damis, p. 55.
42 San Martín, p. 105, Besenyő (2009), pp. 86–94; Damis, pp. 59–73.
43 Hodges, pp. 241–255; Thompson, Adloff, pp. 269–289.
44 Besenyő (2009), pp. 114–122.
45 Anthony H. Cordesman, Arleigh A. Burke and Aram Nerguizian, *The North African Military Balance: Force Developments & Regional Challenges* (CSIS, 7 December 2010), p. 98; Sylvio de Souza Ferreira, 'A experiência de observador militar da ONU no Saara Ocidental', *Conjuntura Austral*, vol. 8, issue 39–40 (dez. 2016/mar. 2017), pp. 27–28.
46 José Maria Sydow de Barros, 'Western Sahara: History, UN acting and foreign interests', *Brazilian Journal of African Studies*, vol. 5, issue 10. (July/December 2020), https://europub.co.uk/articles/western-sahara-history-un-acting-and-foreign-interests-A-692940 (accessed 19 May 2022), p. 110.
47 Jensen, p. 33.
48 Ian Campell Gordon, 'Australians in Western Sahara', *Australian Defence Forces Journal*, issue 104 (January/February 1994), p. 83 and Major Susan Lee Felsche, *Royal Australian Army Medical Corps*, Canberra Doctor (September 2017).
49 Besenyő (2009), pp. 125–131.

Chapter 2

1 Toby Shelley, *Endgame in the Western Sahara: What Future for Africa's Last Colony* (London, New York: Zed Books, 2004), p. 46.; Issaka K. Souaré,'Western Sahara. Is there light at the end of the tunnel?', *ISS Paper 155*, November 2007, https://www.files.ethz.ch/isn/98919/OP155.pdf, accessed 19 May 2022.
2 Jensen. p. 39.; Zunes, Mundy, pp. 182–185.
3 N. F. James, 'Brief History of Australian peacekeeping', *Australian Defence Forces Journal*, issue 104 (January/February 1994), p. 12.
4 János Besenyő, *A nyugat-szaharai válság. Egy magyar békefenntartó szemével* (Pécs: IDResearch Kft/Publikon Kiadó, 2012), pp. 159–165.
5 Anon., 'Un Descendant au Sahara Occidental, par le capitane Michel Barbaize', *La Kouma, 42' ANNÉE, No. 157* (2000), https://lakoumia.fr/images/bulletins/LA%20KOUMIA%20numero%20157.pdf, accessed 19 May 2022, pp. 31–36; William H. Lewis, *Military implications of United Nations peacekeeping operations* (Washington D. C: The Institute for National Strategic Studies, June 1993), p. 62.; George A. Pickart, *The Western Sahara: The Referendum Process in Danger: a Staff Report to the Committee on Foreign Relations of the United States Senate*, United States. (Congress. Senate. Committee on Foreign Relations, 1992), p. 7.
6 James, p. 12. and Gordon, p. 83.
7 MINURSO's initial budget was US$200 million and total personnel of 1,695 (all ranks) including: 550 military observers, an infantry battalion of 700 (all ranks), an air support group of 110 (all ranks) to operate and maintain four fixed-wing aircraft and eight transport helicopters, a signals unit of 45 (all ranks), a medical unit of 50 (all ranks), a composite military police company of 40 (all ranks) and a logistics battalion of 200 (all ranks). Unfortunately, the mission never reached this strength. S/22464, The situation concerning Western Sahara-report by the Secretary-General, 19 April 1991, p. 11.
8 S/22464, The situation concerning Western Sahara-report by the Secretary-General, 19 April 1991, p. 11.
9 William C. Spracher, 'Seeking Cultural Intelligence in the Desert's Shifting Sands While Keeping Peace Along the Berm', *American Intelligence Journal*, vol. 30, issue 1 (2012), https://www.jstor.org/stable/26201991, accessed 19 May 2022, p. 109.
10 Pickart, p. 5.
11 The Center on International Cooperation: Global Peace Operations, ANNUAL REVIEW OF 2006 (2006), p. 119.
12 Gordon, p. 83.
13 Pickart, p. 8.
14 Pickart, p. 5.
15 Spracher, pp. 109–110.
16 Anon., 'YO FUI CASCO AZUL EN EL SAHARA (por el Comodoro VGM (R) Carlos Fernando VIÑAS)', February 2021, https://aevyca.com.ar/wp-content/uploads/2021/02/Yo-fui-Casco-Azul-en-el-Sahara.pdf, accessed 18 May 2022.
17 Gordon, pp. 83–84. Interestingly, at the beginning of the mission, the Canadian commander of the military contingent proposed that the official language of the mission be French, but this was not supported by the UN, so the official language of the mission remained English. Spracher, p. 112.
18 Pickart, pp. 6–7 and 9.
19 Gordon, p. 84.
20 Police Colonel Lajos Tószegi also reported similar experiences, according to which the Moroccan authorities searched his hotel room several times and spied on him. János Besenyő, *Magyar békefenntartók Afrikában* (Budapest: Katonai Nemzetbiztonsági Szolgálat kiadványa, 2013), pp. 50–65.
21 Spracher, p. 13.
22 Joseph Alfred Grinblat, 'My Work on the Origins of Minurso, the UN Mission in Western Sahara', 27 October 2021, https://www.passblue.com/2021/10/27/my-work-on-the-origins-of-minurso-the-un-mission-in-western-sahara/, accessed 18 May 2022.
23 Pickart, p. 5; Norrie Macqueen, *United Nations Peacekeeping in Africa since 1960* (London: Routledge, Taylor and Francis, 2014), pp. 65–66.
24 Spracher, pp. 106–107; Pickart, p. 9.
25 Anon., 'Un Descendant...'
26 Lewis, p. 64; Pickart, pp. 6 and 10.
27 Anon., 'MINURSO: Testimonio de una mujer de Montenegro', *Maghreb online*, 10 July 2021, https://moroccomail.fr/2021/10/07/minurso-testimonio-de-una-mujer-de-montenegro/, accessed 19 May 2022.
28 Pickart, p. 9.
29 William J. Durch (ed.), *The Evolution of UN Peacekeeping, Case Studies, and Comparative Analysis* (New York: St. Martin's Press, 1993), pp. 427–429.; Grinblat, 'My Work on the Origins …'
30 Jacob A. Mundy, '"Seized of the Matter": The UN and the Western Sahara Dispute', *Mediterranean Quarterly*, vol. 15, issue 3 (2004), pp. 131–132; Pickart, pp. 3–4.
31 Jensen, p. 74.

32 Javier Pérez De Cuellar, *Pilgrimage for peace: a Secretary-General's memoir* (New York: St. Martin's Press, 1997), p. 349.
33 Lewis, pp. 62–63.
34 S/25170, The situation concerning Western Sahara-report by the Secretary-General, 26 January 1993.
35 János Besenyő and Péter Miletics, *Országismertető. Marokkó és Nyugat-Szahara* (Budapest: Honvéd Vezérkar Tudományos Kutatóhely, a Katonai Nemzetbiztonsági Szolgálat és a Magyar Honvédség Geoinformációs Szolgálat kiadványa, 2017), pp. 371–374.
36 Jarat Chopra, 'A Chance for Peace in Western Sahara', *Survival*, vol. 39, issue 3 (1997), p. 57.
37 Anna Theofilopoulou, 'The United Nations and Western Sahara. A Never-ending Affair.', *United States Institute of Peace, Special Report*, July 2006, http://www.usip.org/files/resources/sr166.pdf, accessed 18 May 2022; Dunbar, p. 529.
38 de Barros, p. 113.
39 Zunes, Mundy, p. 156; Besenyő (2020), pp. 49–50.
40 Jensen, p. 16.
41 Jensen, pp. 98–99; Dunbar, pp. 528–530.
42 Anna Theofilopoulou, *The United Nations' Change in Approach to Resolving the Western Sahara Conflict Since the turn of the Twenty-First Century*, in Raquel Ojeda-Garcia, Irene Fernández-Molina, Victoria Veguilla (eds.), *Global, Regional and Local Dimensions of Western Sahara's Protracted Decolonisation* (Palgrave Macmillan, 2017), pp. 40–42.
43 Martin Pabs, 'The Western Sahara Conflict', *Scientia Militaria, South African Journal of Military Studies*, Volume 29 (1999), p. 78.
44 S/2000/461, Report of the Secretary-General on the situation concerning Western Sahara, 22 May 2000.
45 Neil Clough, *Western Saharan Conflict: Prolonged Conflict and Prospects for the Future* (thesis, Alabama, Air Command and Staff College, Air University, 2008), pp. 7 and 15.
46 S/2001/613, Report of the Secretary-General on the situation concerning Western Sahara, 20 June 2001.
47 Theofilopoulou (2017), p. 43.
48 S/2002/41, Interim report of the Secretary-General on the situation concerning Western Sahara, 10 January 2002.
49 Besenyő (2020), p. 53.
50 Yahia H. Zoubir, Karima Benabdallah-Gambier, 'The United States and the North African Imbroglio: Balancing Interests in Algeria, Morocco, and the Western Sahara', *Mediterranean Politics*, vol. 10, issue 2 (2005), p. 194–195.
51 S/2003/565, Report of the Secretary-General on the situation concerning Western Sahara, 23 May 2003.
52 Shelley, p. 53–54.
53 Hakim Darbouche, Yahia H. Zoubir, 'Conflicting International Policies and the Western Sahara Stalemate', *The In'ternational Spectator*, vol. 43, issue 1 (2008), p. 93.
54 Zunes, Mundy, p. 239.
55 The Center on International Cooperation: Global Peace Operations, ANNUAL REVIEW OF 2007 (2006), p. 143.
56 György Száraz, 'UN mission in Western Sahara (MINURSO)', in Dr. Gömbös, Ervin (ed.), *The Future of Development Policies and Changing Priorities: Africa* (United Nations Association of Hungary, HUNIDA Kht, 2006) *http://www.menszt.hu/data/le/Publication20060630.pdf*, accessed 18 May 2022, p. 74.
57 Immaculada Szmolka, *Western Sahara and the Arab Spring*, in: Raquel Ojeda-Garcia, Irene Fernández-Molina, Victoria Veguilla, *Global, Regional and Local Dimensions of Western Sahara's Protracted Decolonisation* (Palgrave Macmillan, 2017), p. 101.; Spracher, p. 106.
58 S/2010/175, Report of the Secretary-General on the situation concerning Western Sahara, 6 April 2010.
59 S/2017/307, Report of the Secretary-General on the situation concerning Western Sahara, 10 April 2017.
60 S/2018/889 (3 October 2018).
61 S/2018/277 (29 March 2018).
62 Anon., *January 2019 Monthly Forecast, Security Council Report*, 27 December 2018, https://www.securitycouncilreport.org/monthly-forecast/2019-01/western-sahara.php, accessed 19 May 2022.
63 S/2019/282, Report of the Secretary-General on the situation concerning Western Sahara, 1 April 2019.
64 S/2019/787, Report of the Secretary-General on the situation concerning Western Sahara, 2 October 2019.
65 Anon., *World Peace Foundation: Western Sahara Short Mission Brief*, July 2017, https://sites.tufts.edu/wpf/files/2017/07/Western-Sahara-brief.pdf, accessed 16 May 2022.
66 R. Joseph Huddleston, 'Can John Bolton Thaw Western Sahara's Long-Frozen Conflict?', *Foreign Policy*, 9 May 2019, https://foreignpolicy.com/2019/05/09/can-john-bolton-thaw-western-saharas-long-frozen-conflict-morocco-western-sahara-polisario-minurso-sahrawi-republic/, accessed 16 May 2022.
67 Anon., 'Time for International Re-engagement in Western Sahara', *International Crisis Group*, Briefeing no. 82, 11 March 2021, https://www.crisisgroup.org/middle-east-north-africa/north-africa/western-sahara/b82-time-international-re-engagement-western-sahara, accessed at: 16 May 2022.
68 Anon., 'Things are heating up in Western Sahara', *The Economist*, 6 November 2021, https://www.economist.com/middle-east-and-africa/2021/11/06/things-are-heating-up-in-western-sahara, accessed 18 May 2022; Teresa Nogueira Pinto, 'The fight goes on over Western Sahara's status', *GIS reports online*, 16 May 2022, https://www.gisreportsonline.com/r/western-sahara/, accessed 18 May 2022.
69 Jason Pack, 'Libya's Chaos Is a Warning to the World', *Foreign Policy*, 26 October 2021, https://foreignpolicy.com/2021/10/26/libya-chaos-qaddafi-turkey-uae-france-italy-russia-disorder/, accessed 18 May 2022; A/HRC/49/4, Report of the Independent Fact-Finding Mission on Libya, UN Human Rights Council, 23 March 2022.
70 Heba Saleh, 'Algeria and Morocoo fall out over gas, separatists and Western Sahara', *Financial Times*, 18 October 2021, https://www.ft.com/content/7b21472a-9ffb-44ae-846a-6cc85e228ca6, accessed 18 May 2022.
71 Anthony Dworkin, 'North African standoff: How the Western Sahara conflict is fuelling new tensions between Morocco and Algeria', *European Council on Foreign Relations*, 8 April 2022, https://ecfr.eu/publication/north-african-standoff-how-the-western-sahara-conflict-is-fuelling-new-tensions-between-morocco-and-algeria/, accessed 18 May 2022.
72 Anon., 'Western Sahara', *Security Council Report*, 31 March 2022, https://www.securitycouncilreport.org/monthly-forecast/2022-04/western-sahara-8.php, accessed 18 May 2022.
73 Jacques Rousselier, 'A Role for Russia in the Western Sahara?', *Carnegie Endowment for International Peace*, 05 June 2018, https://carnegieendowment.org/sada/76532, accessed 19 May 2022.
74 Mohamed Alaoui, 'Tensions rise with Morocco as Russia receives Polisario delegation', *The Arab Weekly*, 23 October 2021, https://thearabweekly.com/tensions-rise-morocco-russia-receives-polisario-delegation, accessed 19 May 2022.
75 Khadija Mohsen-Finan, 'Morocco's indignation with Ban Ki-moon: is the Western Sahara an 'occupied' territory?', *Real Instituto Elcano*, 26 July 2016, https://www.realinstitutoelcano.org/en/analyses/moroccos-indignation-with-ban-ki-moon-is-the-western-sahara-an-occupied-territory/, accessed 19 May 2022.
76 Anon., 'New developments around Western Sahara could create an opportunity for Africa to assert its position', *ISS, PSC Report*, 03 June 2016, https://issafrica.org/pscreport/psc-insights/a-new-opportunity-to-assert-africas-role-in-western-sahara, accessed 19 May 2022.
77 Dibie Ike Michael, 'UN mission in Western Sahara renewed for only six months', *Africanews*, 01 November 2018, https://www.africanews.com/2018/11/01/un-mission-in-western-sahara-renewed-for-only-six-months/, accessed 19 May 2022.
78 Sharif Paget, Mitchell McCluskey, 'Western Sahara independence leader declares the end of a 29-year-old ceasefire with Morocco', *CNN.com*, 15 November 2020, https://edition.cnn.com/2020/11/15/world/polisario-front-morocco-western-sahara-ceasefire-intl/index.html, accessed 19 May 2022.
79 Sertan Sanderson, 'Western Sahara: A migrant smuggling hotspot', *Info Migrants*, 22 January 2021, https://www.infomigrants.net/en/post/29818/western-sahara-a-migrant-smuggling-hotspot, accessed 19 May 2022.
80 Conor Gallagher, 'Last two Irish troops withdraw from Western Sahara after 30 years. Defence Forces leave at precarious time for United Nations Minurso mission', *The Irish Times*, 29 July 2021, https://www.irishtimes.com/news/ireland/irish-news/last-two-irish-troops-withdraw-from-western-sahara-after-30-years-1.4633766, accessed 19 May 2022.
81 S/2020/938, The situation concerning Western Sahara-report by the Secretary-General, 23 September 2020.
82 Michäel Tanchum, 'The post-COVID-19 Trajectory for Algeria, Morocco and Western Sahara', *Institutio Affari Internazionali*, 16 January 2021,

https://www.iai.it/en/pubblicazioni/post-covid-19-trajectory-algeria-morocco-and-western-sahara, accessed 20 May 2022.

83 S/2021/843, The situation concerning Western Sahara-report by the Secretary-General, 01 October 2021.

84 S/RES/2602, Resolution 2602, 29 October 2021.

85 Anon., 'How the War in Ukraine May Impact Africa', *Center for Strategic & International Studies*, 1 March 2022, https://www.csis.org/analysis/how-war-ukraine-may-impact-africa, accessed 20 May 2022.

86 Peter Fabricius, 'Ukraine War reveals Africa divided', *Institute for Security Studies*, 18 March 2022, https://issafrica.org/iss-today/ukraine-war-reveals-africa-divided, accessed 20 May 2022.

87 Matthew Lee, 'Blinken urges Algria re-think on Russia, Western Sahara', *AP News*, 30 March 2022, https://apnews.com/article/russia-ukraine-middle-east-africa-antony-blinken-north-africa-f3d4b0be50608327e8cdcc1057bebfe9, accessed 20 May 2022; Martin Jay, 'Blinken's Slick "Diplo Talk" Can't Fix Algeria-Morocco Rift', *Inside Arabia*, 11 April 2022, https://insidearabia.com/blinkens-slick-diplo-talk-cant-fix-algeria-morocco-rift/, accessed 20 May 2022.

88 Anon., 'Morocco scents victory in Western Sahara', *The Economist*, 26 March 2022, https://www.economist.com/middle-east-and-africa/2022/03/26/morocco-scents-victory-in-western-sahara, accessed 20 May 2022.

89 Thomas M. Hill, 'Ukraine War Puts New Focus on Conflict in Western Sahara', *United States Institute of Peace*, 14 April 2022, https://www.usip.org/publications/2022/04/ukraine-war-puts-new-focus-conflict-western-sahara, accessed 20 May 2022.

Chapter 3

1 Anon., *World Peace Foundation: Western Sahara Short Mission Brief*, July 2017, https://sites.tufts.edu/wpf/files/2017/07/Western-Sahara-brief.pdf, accessed 16 May 2022.

2 R. Joseph Huddleston, 'Can John Bolton Thaw Western Sahara's Long-Frozen Conflict?', *Foreign Policy*, 9 May 2019, https://foreignpolicy.com/2019/05/09/can-john-bolton-thaw-western-saharas-long-frozen-conflict-morocco-western-sahara-polisario-minurso-sahrawi-republic/, accessed 16 May 2022.

3 Anon., 'Time for International Re-engagement in Western Sahara', *International Crisis Group*, Briefeing no. 82, 11 March 2021, https://www.crisisgroup.org/middle-east-north-africa/north-africa/western-sahara/b82-time-international-re-engagement-western-sahara, accessed at: 16 May 2022.

4 Anon., 'Things are heating up in Western Sahara', *The Economist*, 6 November 2021, https://www.economist.com/middle-east-and-africa/2021/11/06/things-are-heating-up-in-western-sahara, accessed 18 May 2022; Teresa Nogueira Pinto, 'The fight goes on over Western Sahara's status', *GIS reports online*, 16 May 2022, https://www.gisreportsonline.com/r/western-sahara/, accessed 18 May 2022.

5 Jason Pack, 'Libya's Chaos Is a Warning to the World', *Foreign Policy*, 26 October 2021, https://foreignpolicy.com/2021/10/26/libya-chaos-qaddafi-turkey-uae-france-italy-russia-disorder/, accessed 18 May 2022; A/HRC/49/4, Report of the Independent Fact-Finding Mission on Libya, UN Human Rights Council, 23 March 2022.

6 Heba Saleh, 'Algeria and Morocoo fall out over gas, separatists and Western Sahara', *Financial Times*, 18 October 2021, https://www.ft.com/content/7b21472a-9ffb-44ae-846a-6cc85e228ca6, accessed 18 May 2022.

7 Anthony Dworkin, 'North African standoff: How the Western Sahara conflict is fuelling new tensions between Morocco and Algeria', *European Council on Foreign Relations*, 8 April 2022, https://ecfr.eu/publication/north-african-standoff-how-the-western-sahara-conflict-is-fuelling-new-tensions-between-morocco-and-algeria/, accessed 18 May 2022.

8 Anon., 'Western Sahara', *Security Council Report*, 31 March 2022, https://www.securitycouncilreport.org/monthly-forecast/2022-04/western-sahara-8.php, accessed 18 May 2022.

9 Jacques Rousselier, 'A Role for Russia in the Western Sahara?', *Carnegie Endowment for International Peace*, 05 June 2018, https://carnegieendowment.org/sada/76532, accessed 19 May 2022.

10 Mohamed Alaoui, 'Tensions rise with Morocco as Russia receives Polisario delegation', *The Arab Weekly*, 23 October 2021, https://thearabweekly.com/tensions-rise-morocco-russia-receives-polisario-delegation, accessed 19 May 2022.

11 Khadija Mohsen-Finan, 'Morocco's indignation with Ban Ki-moon: is the Western Sahara an 'occupied' territory?', *Real Instituto Elcano*, 26 July 2016, https://www.realinstitutoelcano.org/en/analyses/moroccos-indignation-with-ban-ki-moon-is-the-western-sahara-an-occupied-territory/, accessed 19 May 2022.

12 Anon., 'New developments around Western Sahara could create an opportunity for Africa to assert its position', *ISS, PSC Report*, 03 June 2016, https://issafrica.org/pscreport/psc-insights/a-new-opportunity-to-assert-africas-role-in-western-sahara, accessed 19 May 2022.

13 Dibie Ike Michael, 'UN mission in Western Sahara renewed for only six months', *Africanews*, 01 November 2018, https://www.africanews.com/2018/11/01/un-mission-in-western-sahara-renewed-for-only-six-months/, accessed 19 May 2022.

14 Sharif Paget, Mitchell McCluskey, 'Western Sahara independence leader declares the end of a 29-year-old ceasefire with Morocco', *CNN.com*, 15 November 2020, https://edition.cnn.com/2020/11/15/world/polisario-front-morocco-western-sahara-ceasefire-intl/index.html, accessed 19 May 2022.

15 Sertan Sanderson, 'Western Sahara: A migrant smuggling hotspot', *Info Migrants*, 22 January 2021, https://www.infomigrants.net/en/post/29818/western-sahara-a-migrant-smuggling-hotspot, accessed 19 May 2022.

16 Conor Gallagher, 'Last two Irish troops withdraw from Western Sahara after 30 years. Defence Forces leave at precarious time for United Nations Minurso mission', *The Irish Times*, 29 July 2021, https://www.irishtimes.com/news/ireland/irish-news/last-two-irish-troops-withdraw-from-western-sahara-after-30-years-1.4633766, accessed 19 May 2022.

17 S/2020/938, The situation concerning Western Sahara-report by the Secretary-General, 23 September 2020.

18 Michäel Tanchum, 'The post-COVID-19 Trajectory for Algeria, Morocco and Western Sahara', *Institutio Affari Internazionali*, 16 January 2021, https://www.iai.it/en/pubblicazioni/post-covid-19-trajectory-algeria-morocco-and-western-sahara, accessed 20 May 2022.

19 S/2021/843, The situation concerning Western Sahara-report by the Secretary-General, 01 October 2021.

20 S/RES/2602, Resolution 2602, 29 October 2021.

21 Anon., 'How the War in Ukraine May Impact Africa', *Center for Strategic & International Studies*, 1 March 2022, https://www.csis.org/analysis/how-war-ukraine-may-impact-africa, accessed 20 May 2022.

22 Peter Fabricius, 'Ukraine War reveals Africa divided', *Institute for Security Studies*, 18 March 2022, https://issafrica.org/iss-today/ukraine-war-reveals-africa-divided, accessed 20 May 2022.

23 Matthew Lee, 'Blinken urges Algria re-think on Russia, Western Sahara', *AP News*, 30 March 2022, https://apnews.com/article/russia-ukraine-middle-east-africa-antony-blinken-north-africa-f3d4b0be50608327e8cdcc1057bebfe9, accessed 20 May 2022; Martin Jay, 'Blinken's Slick "Diplo Talk" Can't Fix Algeria-Morocco Rift', *Inside Arabia*, 11 April 2022, https://insidearabia.com/blinkens-slick-diplo-talk-cant-fix-algeria-morocco-rift/, accessed 20 May 2022.

24 Anon., 'Morocco scents victory in Western Sahara', *The Economist*, 26 March 2022, https://www.economist.com/middle-east-and-africa/2022/03/26/morocco-scents-victory-in-western-sahara, accessed 20 May 2022.

25 Thomas M. Hill, 'Ukraine War Puts New Focus on Conflict in Western Sahara', *United States Institute of Peace*, 14 April 2022, https://www.usip.org/publications/2022/04/ukraine-war-puts-new-focus-conflict-western-sahara, accessed 20 May 2022.

Chapter 4

1 Anon., *Office Locations, MINURSO homepage*, https://minurso.unmissions.org/office-locations, accessed 28 June 2022.

2 Anon., *MINURSO fact sheet, MINURSO homepage*, https://peacekeeping.un.org/en/mission/minurso, accessed 28 June 2022.

3 Anon., *Ceasefire monitoring, MINURSO homepage*, https://minurso.unmissions.org/ceasefire-monitoring, accessed 28 June 2022.

4 Anon., *Troop and police contributors, MINURSO homepage*, https://peacekeeping.un.org/en/troop-and-police-contributors, accessed 28 June 2022.

5 Anon., *Ceasefire monitoring, MINURSO homepage*, https://minurso.unmissions.org/ceasefire-monitoring, accessed 28 June 2022.

6 Spracher, p. 109; Philippe D. Rogers, 'China and United Nations Peacekeeping Operations in Africa', *Naval War College Review*, vol. 60, issue 2, article 7 (2007), https://digital-commons.usnwc.edu/nwc-review/vol60/iss2/7, accessed 19 May 2022.

7 S/2005/648, Report of the Secretary-General on the situation concerning Western Sahara, 13 October 2005.

8 de Barros, p. 114.

9 Száraz, p. 73; YO FUI CASCO …

10 S/1998/35, Report of the Secretary-General on the Situation Concerning Western Sahara, 15 January 1998.
11 S/1999/307, Report of the Secretary-General on the Situation Concerning Western Sahara, 22 March 1999; Macqueen, p. 245.
12 Lewis, p. 65; YO FUI CASCO...; Cai Shihao, Liang Ying and Tai Beiping, 'Surviving in the sand', *China Daily*, 21 December 2007, https://www.chinadaily.com.cn/cndy/2007-12/21/content_6337521.htm, accessed 18 May 2022; Ferreira, p. 36.
13 Spracher, p. 112.
14 YO FUI CASCO ...
15 Száraz, pp. 71–72.
16 Anon., *Mine action, MINURSO homepage*, https://minurso.unmissions.org/mine-action, accessed 28 June 2022.
17 Spracher, pp. 111 and 113.
18 S/1994/283, The situation concerning Western Sahara-report by the Secretary-General, 10 March 1994.
19 S/24040, The situation concerning Western Sahara-report by the Secretary-General, 29 May 1992 and Lewis, p. 63.
20 S/25170, The situation concerning Western Sahara-report by the Secretary-General, 26 January 1993.
21 YO FUI CASCO ...
22 S/26797, The situation concerning Western Sahara-report by the Secretary-General, 24 November 1993; Gordon, p. 85. and Major Felsche, p. 3.
23 S/1994/283, The situation concerning Western Sahara-report by the Secretary-General, 10 March 1994.
24 S/1994/819, The situation concerning Western Sahara-report by the Secretary-General, 12 July 1994.
25 S/1994/1257, The situation concerning Western Sahara-report by the Secretary-General, 5 November 1994.
26 S/2006/817, Report of the Secretary-General on the situation concerning Western Sahara, 16 October 2006, and Anon., 'After 12 years, Korean medical unit departs UN mission in Western Sahara', *UN News*, 15 May 2006, https://news.un.org/en/story/2006/05/178832-after-12-years-korean-medical-unit-departs-un-mission-western-sahara, accessed 28 June 2022.
27 Anon., 'MINURSO farewell Malaysian Medical Unit, welcome Bangladeshi Medical Unit', *MINURSO homepage*, 15 December 2010, https://minurso.unmissions.org/minurso-farewell-malaysian-medical-unit-welcome-bangladeshi-medical-unit, accessed 28 June 2022.
28 S/2011/249, Report of the Secretary-General on the situation concerning Western Sahara, 1 April 2011.
29 Sara E. Davies, Simon Rushton, 'Healing or Harming? United Nations Peacekeeping and Health' (New York: International Peace Institute, March 2015) https://www.ipinst.org/wp-content/uploads/2015/03/IPI_Rpt_Health_and_Peacekeeping.pdf, accessed 28 June 2022.
30 Anon., 'MINURSO The United Nations Mission for the Referendum in Western Sahara: Der Weg zum VN-Militärbeobachter – Teil 3', Mahbas, 16 October 2020, https://www.bundeswehr.de/de/einsaetze-bundeswehr/die-bundeswehr-in-marokko/einsatz-minurso-vn-militaebeobachter-westsahara-3555412, accessed 28 June 2022.
31 MINURSO has 3 MI-8 helicopters, three An-26 and one An-24 aircraft. They are used to carry out the logistical service of the camps, the transport of peacekeepers, CASEVAC and MEDEVAC activities, as well as air patrolling. Although it was previously suggested that another type of aircraft (DHC-6 Twin Otter) would be used for the operation, the Russian aircraft remained due to their cheapness and reliability. Anon., *Review of Aviation Safety in the Department of Peacekeeping Operations, United Nations Archives*, https://search.archives.un.org/uploads/r/united-nations-archives /d/7/6/d765b92a3231ea25aba82ddf7aa83a5d681b0adf1ec152c95fc186fffee35b00/S-1092-0102-06-00012.pdf, accessed 28 June 2022.
32 Anon., 'Un Descendant' pp. 31–36.
33 The Center on International Cooperation: Global Peace Operations, ANNUAL REVIEW OF 2006 (2006), p. 135.
34 Száraz, p. 73; Ferreira, p. 38; Rogers.
35 Pickart, p. 6.
36 S/1996/674, Progress Report of the Secretary-General on the Situation Concerning Western Sahara, 20 August 1996.
37 The Center on International Cooperation: Global Peace Operations, ANNUAL REVIEW OF 2006 (2006), p. 119.
38 A significant part of the information about the Moroccan Armed Forces and the Polisario Front comes from the information the author obtained during his time in the mission, as well as from interviews with MINURSO military observers and police officers who later served there, from the Recognition Handbook, Western Sahara Region published by the Canadian government, and from: Anon., *Foro de Inteligencia, Espionaje y Servicios Secretos Foro sobre: Inteligencia, Espionaje y Servicios Secretos*, http://www.intelpage.info/forum/viewtopic.php?t=132, accessed 19 May 2022 and Anon., *skyscrapercity.com/Moroccan Air Armed Forces*, http://www.skyscrapercity.com/showthread.php?t=442085, accessed 19 May 2022.
39 Anthony H. Cordesman, *A Tragedy of Arms, Military and Security Developments in the Maghreb* (Westport, Conn.: Praeger, 2002), p. 613.
40 Interview with a peacekeeper serving in the MINURSO operation, who did not wish to disclose their nationality and rank.
41 This problem occurs with all opposing parties. Right from the beginning of the mission, it happened that the opposing parties did not cooperate properly with the peacekeepers, or even hindered their work. Lewis, pp. 64–65.
42 Anon., *World Peace Foundation: Western Sahara Short Mission Brief*, July 2017, https://sites.tufts.edu/wpf/files/2017/07/Western-Sahara-brief.pdf, accessed 16 May 2022; Pickart, pp. 8, 11.
43 S/1996/913, Report of the Secretary-General on the Situation Concerning Western Sahara, 5 November 1996.
44 The Center on International Cooperation: Global Peace Operations, ANNUAL REVIEW OF 2006 (2006), p. 119.
45 Anon., *Ceasefire monitoring, MINURSO homepage*, https://minurso.unmissions.org/ceasefire-monitoring, accessed 28 June 2022.
46 Zunes, Mundy, p. 27.
47 Interview with a peacekeeper serving in the MINURSO operation, who did not wish to disclose their nationality and rank.
48 Very little is known about the real number of Moroccan troops stationed on the wall system. It is estimated that at least 120,000 Moroccan soldiers are in the 'Southern Zone' supported by 29,000 paramilitary gendarmerie forces (Gendarmerie Royale), 25,000 border guards and 5,000-man Mobile Intervention Companies. Cordesman, Burke and Nerguizian (2010), *The North African*, p. 98.
49 Anon., *Akhbar Es-Sahra (News of The Sahara), Western Sahara Mission UK & Ireland*, Newsletter N°2, 10 January 2002, http://www.arso.org/akhbar2.htm, accessed 28 June 2022.
50 Anon., 'Paris-Dakar Rally Driver Hits Land Mine', *ABC News*, 8 January 2001, http://abcnews.go.com/International/story?id=81746&page=1, accessed 28 June 2022.
51 Anouar Boukhars, 'The drivers of insecurity in Mauritania', *The Carnegie Papers*, April 2012, https://carnegieendowment.org/files/mauritania_insecurity.pdf, accessed 28 June 2022; Salem, 'Rethinking the weak state paradigm'.
52 S/1994/819, The situation concerning Western Sahara-report by the Secretary-General, 12 July 1994.
53 S/24464, Letter Dated 31 August 1992 from the President of the Security Council Addressed to the Secretary-General, 31 August 1992.
54 Interview with Major Tamás Hárs, who served as a peacekeeper in the MINURSO staff. Besenyő (2013), pp. 86–95.
55 I gained many a pleasant experience in this camp, as I started my service here under the command of Major Béla Tamási, who was feared and admired by the peacekeepers and nicknamed 'the Hungarian Terminator.' The Major became the commander of the most neglected and undisciplined camp of the mission, where in a short time he worked almost miracles with the soldiers assigned to him, so the camp soon became the best camp of the mission. After he had gone to Tindouf, some of the peacekeepers who had been under strict discipline until then tried to take revenge on me – as the only Hungarian soldier (a young captain) available in a radius of hundreds of kilometres. Of course, this period ended quickly, so I was appreciated for my own work, not for what the lieutenant colonel did, although his work was still spoken of in superlatives at the general headquarters for a long time.
56 Anon., *Ceasefire monitoring, MINURSO homepage*, https://minurso.unmissions.org/ceasefire-monitoring, accessed 28 June 2022.
57 Anthony H. Cordesman, Aram Nerguizian, *The North African military balance: force development in the Maghreb* (Washington D.C.: CSIS Press, 2009), p. 28–31.; Yago Rodrigues, The Armoured Force of the Moroccan Army, Ejercitos, 29/09/2018, https://www.revistaejercitos.com/en/2018/09/29/the-armored-force-of-the-morocco-army/ accessed 28 June 2022.; Royal Moroccan Army – Order of Battle, GlobalSecurity.org, https://www.globalsecurity.org/military/world/morocco/army-orbat.htm accessed 28 June 2022.
58 Anon., *Ceasefire monitoring, MINURSO homepage*, https://minurso.unmissions.org/ceasefire-monitoring, accessed 28 June 2022.

59 S/23662, Report of the Secretary-General on the United Nations Mission for the Referendum in Western Sahara, 28 February 1992.
60 S/26797, The situation concerning Western Sahara-report by the Secretary-General, 24 November 1993.
61 Anon., *Ceasefire monitoring, MINURSO homepage*, https://minurso.unmissions.org/ceasefire-monitoring, accessed 28 June 2022.
62 S/2010/175, Report of the Secretary-General on the situation concerning Western Sahara, 6 April 2010.
63 Száraz, p. 69.
64 Spracher, p. 108.
65 Nassrine Azimi, *The Role and Functions of the Civilian Police in the United Nations Peace-keeping Operations* (The Hague: Kluwer Law International, 1996), p. 107–111.
66 Roxane D. V. Sismanidis, *Police Functions in Peace Operation, Report from Workshop organised by the United States Institute of Peace*, p. 3.
67 S/26797, The situation concerning Western Sahara-report by the Secretary-General, 24 November 1993.
68 S/1994/283, The situation concerning Western Sahara-report by the Secretary-General, 10 March 1994.
69 S/1994/1257, The situation concerning Western Sahara-report by the Secretary-General, 5 November 1994.
70 Glassner, p. 270.
71 S/1995/240, The situation concerning Western Sahara-report by the Secretary-General, 30 March 1995.
72 S/1995/404, The situation concerning Western Sahara-report by the Secretary-General, 19 May 1995.
73 S/1995/779, The situation concerning Western Sahara-report by the Secretary-General, 8 September 1995.
74 S/1996/43, Report of the Secretary-General on the Situation Concerning Western Sahara, 19 January 1996.
75 S/1996/343, Report of the Secretary-General on the Situation Concerning Western Sahara, 8 May 1996.
76 Azimi, p. 108–110.
77 S/1996/674, Progress Report of the Secretary-General on the Situation Concerning Western Sahara, 20 August 1996.
78 S/1997/166, Letter Dated 10 March 1997 from the Permanent Representative of Morocco to the United Nations Addressed to the President of the Security Council, 10 March 1997.
79 S/1997/358, Report of the Secretary-General on the Situation Concerning Western Sahara, 5 May 1997.
80 S/1997/742, Report of the Secretary-General on the Situation Concerning Western Sahara, 24 September 1997.
81 S/1998/35, Report of the Secretary-General on the Situation Concerning Western Sahara, 15 January 1998.
82 S/1998/775, Progress Report of the Secretary-General on the Situation Concerning Western Sahara, 18 August 1998.
83 S/1999/307, Report of the Secretary-General on the Situation Concerning Western Sahara, 22 March 1999.
84 S/1999/1219, Report of the Secretary-General on the Situation Concerning Western Sahara, 6 December 1999.
85 S/2000/1029, Report of the Secretary-General on the Situation Concerning Western Sahara, 25 October 2000.
86 S/2003/1016, Report of the Secretary-General on the Situation Concerning Western Sahara, 16 October 2003.
87 S/2004/39, Report of the Secretary-General on the Situation Concerning Western Sahara, 19 January 2004.
88 S/2005/254, Report of the Secretary-General on the Situation Concerning Western Sahara, 19 April 2005.
89 Besenyő (2009), p. 159.
90 Anon., *MINURSO fact sheet, MINURSO homepage*, https://peacekeeping.un.org/en/mission/minurso, accessed 28 June 2022.

About the Author

János Besenyő is a professor in Óbuda University (Hungary) and head of the Africa Research Institute. Between 1987 and 2018, he worked as a professional soldier and served in several peace operations in Africa and Afghanistan. He received a PhD in military science from Zrínyi Miklós National Defense University and a habilitated doctorate at Eötvös Lóránd University. In 2014, he established the Scientific Research Center of the Hungarian Defence Forces General Staff, and was its first leader from 2014 to 2018. His most recent publication is *Darfur Peacekeepers: The African Union Peacekeeping Mission in Darfur (AMIS) from the Perspective of a Hungarian Military Advisor.*